Doing English Language

A guide for students

Angela Goddard

Routledge
Taylor & Francis Group

LONDON AND NEW YORK

First published 2012
by Routledge
2 Park Square, Milton Park, Abingdon, Oxon OX14 4RN

Simultaneously published in the USA and Canada
by Routledge
711 Third Avenue, New York, NY 10017

*Routledge is an imprint of the Taylor & Francis Group,
an informa business*

British Library Cataloguing in Publication Data
A catalogue record for this book is available from the British Library

Library of Congress Cataloging in Publication Data
Goddard, Angela, 1954–
Doing English language: a guide for students / Angela Goddard.
p. cm.
Includes bibliographical references and index.
1. English language – Study and teaching – Foreign speakers. I. Title.
PE1128.G54 2012
428.2'4 – dc23
2011041610

ISBN 13: 978-0-415-61883-0 (hbk)
ISBN 13: 978-0-415-61882-3 (pbk)

Typeset in Times
by RefineCatch Limited, Bungay, Suffolk

Printed and bound in Great Britain by
TJ International Ltd, Padstow, Cornwall

Doing English Language

Doing English Language provides a concise, lively and accessible introduction to the field of English Language studies for readers who are interested in taking courses at university level.

This book addresses the fundamental questions about studying English Language, including:

- How is English Language studied and researched?
- Which subject areas does English Language draw on?
- How are different topics approached?
- How is the study of English Language relevant to real world contexts?
- What careers can English Language lead to?

Written by an experienced teacher, researcher, and examiner, *Doing English Language* is both an essential guide for students at pre-university stage and a course companion for undergraduates choosing options within a degree programme.

Angela Goddard is a Professor of English Language, formerly at York St John University, UK, a Higher Education Academy National Teaching Fellow, and Chair of Examiners for English Language A Level at a UK national examination board.

Contents

List of illustrations

Figures

Tables

Preface

In 2011, I overheard a conversation in a pizza shop in a small town in Sweden, between two young men, one Swedish and one German. They were both speaking English and agreeing that their knowledge of English had helped them feel at home in lots of different places across Europe and beyond. They also talked about how different English is in different parts of the world. There was a pause while they companionably munched their pizzas and checked their mobile phones, then one of them asked the other, 'Have you ever been to England? They speak *really* weird English there.'

I loved this statement for a number of reasons. It means that lots of other people now have a stake in the English language and so people like me no longer have to live up to some kind of mythical native-speaker genius. I loved the confidence with which the young man pronounced on the weirdness of English in England, and I wondered what had led him to this view – was it the accents he encountered, or some dialect words, or some of the routines people go in for in the UK, like talking about the weather? As an academic, I wanted to quiz him about his experiences – but of course he would have been very polite and apologetic, and I would have had to admit I was eavesdropping. More than anything, I was intrigued at the thought that after a lifetime of hearing learners of English as a second language apologising for their poor language skills, I might see my own language become a quaint regional dialect of European English.

I offer this anecdote as a kind of snapshot of the tremendous changes that are happening to English world-wide, and as evidence that the study of English

Language is a topical, relevant, and rewarding activity which is about real people and their behaviour. But you don't have to go abroad to get this kind of insight: new technologies are enabling connections with people we would never previously have met. It is a fascinating time for anyone interested in language and communication.

The study of English Language as a school subject has a complex history, which is unpicked a little in the early chapters of this book. But by far the most significant development over the past 20 years has been the steady growth in numbers of students taking courses in English Language at AS/A Level. This book is aimed at students who want to study English Language at higher education level – whether as a continuation from school or college courses, or as a new venture altogether.

University courses have responded to student interest in English Language in different ways, and that fact alone justifies this book. English Language at degree level clearly shares some common ground with Linguistics, but for many departments, English Language is a genuinely interdisciplinary subject that can also embrace aspects of English Literature, Media and Cultural Studies, Creative Writing, and more. Interdisciplinarity of this kind is exciting, but can be very confusing for a student applicant trying to understand the nature of a particular degree course. This book will help readers to understand how English Language can draw on diverse academic fields. The book will act as a guide not just for new applicants but for undergraduates who are continuing to make choices between different pathways of study.

The chapters of this book refer specifically to the benchmarks for English Language produced in 2011 to describe courses of study at UK universities. During the course of the book, there is an incremental account of the different skills that studying English Language should develop. However, for those who are unsure at the outset what those skills are, I offer my own digest below. It will be a good test of this book, and of the subject it describes, if by the end you are convinced that a course of study in English Language could help you to develop the following:

Critical skills

A workplace needs employees who can stand back from what is going on and take an analytical view – that is a critical skill fundamental to research in English Language. Researching something in an organisation – for example, how processes work, or how to change a system, or how to start a new project – entails a number of steps. The first step is some critical thinking in order to work out what the research question is. English Language students are used to dealing with complexity, and looking at issues from different angles, because issues of language are complex and the whole subject is interdisciplinary.

Data collection skills

English Language students know about data, in all its forms. Working with human participants and looking at aspects of communication require an understanding of the different sources of information that can be called 'data'. English Language students have particular awareness of different types of text, and skills in how to sort and sift information, understanding that there is no one version of 'the truth'.

Presentation skills

If English Language study teaches us anything, it is about the power of language to construct views and attitudes. In studying processes of language understanding and how different texts and discourses work, English Language students are well placed to put their insights to use in their own presentations. They should be particularly skilled in constructing cogent arguments and aware of the language aspects of new communication technologies.

Communication skills

Presenting ideas counts as communication, but there are other aspects to communication as well. Listening skills are very important, not just in order to hear others' views, but in order to understand why they hold those views. English Language students become expert at 'reading between the lines' of what is said and what is meant. This is a key skill for negotiations.

Intercultural skills

English Language students know how language and culture are strongly connected, and how many assumptions can be in play when people interact. In our globalised world, different cultural groups are in contact as never before. Changes to the English language itself are underway as new varieties emerge from these new levels of connectedness. If anyone can help us understand the communication processes of our contemporary world, it's a student of English Language.

Angela Goddard
York, 2011

Acknowledgements

Thanks to: Adrian Beard, Beverly Geesin, Chris Hall, and Nikki Swift for their contributions and comments on drafts and to the LINC Tameside Secondary Working Party, 1990–92, for the 'Argument' texts.

The author and publishers would like to thank the following copyright holders for permission to reproduce the extracts from the following:

BBC News Website (2011), 'Viewpoint: Why do some Americanisms irritate people?', 13 July.

Figure 4.2, 'T-shirt, I Saw, I Conquered, I Came'. Reproduced with kind permission of Taiche, http://www.redbubble.com/people/taiche/t-shirts/2559139-i-saw-i-conquered-i-came.

Pret a Manger napkin extract. Reproduced with kind permission of Pret a Manger Ltd.

Figures 5.4, 5.4, 5.6, and 6.2, from *99 Ways to Tell a Story: Exercises in Style* by Matt Madden, published by Jonathan Cape. Reproduced by permission of The Random House Group Ltd.

Extracts from *99 Ways to Tell a Story: Exercises in Style* by Matt Madden, copyright (c) 2005 by Matt Madden. Used by permission of Chamberlain Bros. a division of Penguin Group (USA) Inc.

Figures 5.9 and 5.10, Wall Street Institute 'I'm Cool' and 'I'm Hot' images. Reproduced courtesy of Wall Street Institute, Thailand.

Pages 56 and 57 from 'What Do Graduates Do?' (2010) © HECSU/AGSAS. Reproduced with kind permission of Graduate Prospects Ltd.

While the publishers have made every effort to contact copyright holders of material used in this volume, they would be grateful to hear from any they were unable to contact.

Note on the text

Capitalised names refer to areas of study, for example, English Language, Linguistics, English Literature, Media Studies, Creative Writing.

Use of lower case refers to other aspects, for example, 'English language' means the language itself; 'linguistic' means language-related; 'literature' refers to literary texts, or academic writing in general; 'creative writing' refers to the activity of writing.

Emboldened terms are explained in the combined Index and Glossary at the back of the book.

Introduction

What is 'English'?

In theory, this should be an easy question to answer – it's a language. However, if you ask that question in the context of education, thinking about what is taught and learnt under that heading, the answer is a lot more complicated, largely because 'English' has meant something very different at different times in history, as well as varying in nature from place to place.

This book is a companion volume to Robert Eaglestone's *Doing English*, also published by Routledge (Eaglestone 2002). Eaglestone's book is very similar in aim to this one, in that it attempts to help students understand more about the subject they are thinking of studying in UK higher education. But there is one big difference: this book is about the study of language, not literature. *Doing English* carries the sub-heading *A Guide for Literature Students* on the front cover, to make sure that readers understand that 'English' means 'just literature'. But the suggestion that 'English' can exclude the study of language shows something of the complex history of the subject area.

Chapters 1 and 2 of this book will set out some of the factors that have shaped the identity of 'English' as a subject within the UK. Later chapters will look in some detail at contemporary English Language study, at the different subjects that have contributed to it, at how it can be applied to other academic disciplines, and how it can be researched. Chapters 10 and 11 point readers towards career paths that are particularly well suited to candidates with an English Language background.

This book focuses primarily on the UK context, but of course no country or culture operates in isolation. Academic communities engage in international dialogues and this process has accelerated rapidly with the development of the internet and other digital communication systems. At different times, fields of scholarship that developed in one country have become very influential in another, and there are several examples of this throughout this book. If you are reading this book from the perspective of learning or teaching about English outside of the UK, there will be some important points of reference for your understanding of how particular curricula or approaches have developed in your own local context. Also, because of the growth of English as a global language and the recognition of different 'Englishes', there are ongoing world-wide changes to English both as a subject of study and as a communication medium that are highly relevant to international readers.

1

Where did the study of English Language come from?

The study of English Language, like the study of English Literature, has developed only relatively recently at university level in the UK. Until the very end of the nineteenth century, there was no such subject as 'English' in universities, and students who wanted to study the language and literature of a culture took 'Classics' – the language and literature of Ancient Greece and Rome, civilisations that were much admired and imitated throughout the Western world. Early attitudes to what was deemed 'respectable' within the area of English study can be seen in a pamphlet produced in 1887 by Henry Nettleships, an Oxford University Professor of Classics. This pamphlet, entitled *The Study of Modern European Languages and Literatures at the University of Oxford*, rejected the study of English Literature as in any way comparable to Classics, but saw **philology** – the study of the history of language – as just about acceptable. However, philology, as conceived then, was not about the real language of contemporary English speakers or about any aspects of social history (such as language for new inventions or new experiences). It was described as a 'science', looking at the history of specific language features. Think of philology as comparable to the classification of types of insect (entomology) or plants and flowers (botany), where scholars work to categorise and label types and sub-types.

While the study of English Literature at university level was rapidly established during the twentieth century, particularly after the First World War (1914–18), the study of English Language at that same level never really acquired an independent existence until more recently. However, UK universities have not been the only site of debate about the nature of English Language.

In the broader educational world beyond universities, nineteenth-century Britain was a time of rapid social change. In particular, the Elementary Education Act of 1870 resulted in compulsory schooling for children aged 5–12, and by 1880, 3,000–4,000 schools had opened or had been taken over by School Boards (Stephens 1998). So beyond the formal study of English Language at university level, there were some fundamental issues about what kind of language should be taught and learnt within the school system, both in the UK and further afield, across the British Empire.

The beginnings of universal schooling in the UK coincided (not accidentally) with the establishment of a number of powerful groups whose aim was to preserve the idea of national heritage. So, for example, while the new National Trust saw its role to preserve culturally significant landmarks, the English Association (established in 1907) saw its role as rather similar – to promote English Language as a kind of gateway for appreciating 'great literary works'. The idea was that English Language would be a cultural vehicle for the transmission of the values of the ruling elite, not as a medium for ordinary individuals to use for self-expression and personal identity. The latter idea is much more recent.

Teachers of English language in the early days of compulsory education were seen as 'speech missionaries' in the UK as well across the British Empire. In India, an Education Act in 1835 required Indian schools to use English as the medium of instruction. In the UK, the issue was also about requiring new forms of language to be learnt by those being newly schooled – but this time it was about requiring regional, working-class English speakers to acquire Standard English vocabulary and grammar, and to change their accents to **Received Pronunciation** (RP), the prestige accent which had developed in the English public schools, the universities of Oxford and Cambridge, and therefore all the main offices of Church and State. In order to justify this idea, powerful figures in society frequently portrayed the language of UK regional, working-class speakers as inadequate. They were considered to have a poor vocabulary:

> A country Clergyman informed me that he believed the labourers in his parish had not 300 words in their vocabulary, and a recent article in the Quarterly extends the statements to the great mass of our rural population.
>
> (D'Orsey 1861)

Regional language was often described as corrupting, degenerate and abnormal:

'The language is going to pieces before our eyes, especially under the influence of the debased dialect of the Cockney, which is spreading from our schools and training colleges all over the country' (Ratcliffe 1909).

'Manchester children ... spoke the perverted Lancashire dialect of the towns, had a narrow vocabulary, and could not understand diction' (Shawcross, Chairman of the Examination Board of the National Union of Teachers 1909).

On reading these quotes, you might be thinking that although the language of the complaints has been toned down a bit, not that much has actually changed. You could argue that in the UK there is still a lot of prejudice about regional language and that the false idea of Standard English as a superior form of language use continues to have some currency. The point is that studying English Language now includes focusing precisely on such issues, analysing the factors involved, and trying to understand how present attitudes to language have arisen. This is not all that the study of English Language is about, however.

Scholarship in the area of English Language is also interested in *using* language, as some of the university departments that currently house degree level work include modules on professional writing in all its forms. Again, a historical dimension and a focus on the education system can help explain this emphasis. In the early days of compulsory schooling, English Language was conceived as a medium for admiring literature, and for learning about the values of the ruling classes, not about individual creativity or expression. Over the years, there have been many debates and contested ideas about what exactly the school curriculum for English should include, and many official reports on that subject have been issued (for example, the Newbolt Report in 1921, the Bullock Report in 1975, the Kingman Report in 1988). Gradually, the idea of acquiring skills in English in order to be an effective communicator – not simply in order to write about literature – has gained ground within the school system, and this has had a knock-on effect within higher education. A very recent development – that of the emergence of Creative Writing courses in universities – can be seen as one outcome of this process.

The phrase 'creative writing' used to be associated with literary authors and texts, but now often has a much wider meaning of innovative and original writing in any **genre** or format. Undoubtedly, the rise of Web 2.0 technologies, with users now able to create their own digital compositions, has brought a new dynamism to the whole area.

2

Where did the subject of Linguistics come from?

The answer to this question depends on two things: (1) your cultural perspective; and (2) your definition of Linguistics, particularly how you see the difference between Linguistics and other subject areas. These two aspects are interconnected, as you will see below.

European academics looking for a modern starting point for Linguistics tend to refer particularly to the work of a twentieth-century Swiss scholar called Ferdinand de Saussure and to his *Course in General Linguistics* which was repeatedly delivered between 1907 and 1911 at the University of Geneva. His lectures were published posthumously in 1916 and have since been re-published many times (for example, de Saussure 1974). Some of de Saussure's central concepts spread well beyond Linguistics to have a strong influence on other areas, where they have had a lasting effect. For example, his term and concept – **semiology** (also now referred to as **semiotics**) – has heavily influenced work in Media Studies and is still current. More will be said about his influential concepts in Chapters 4 and 5.

The European tradition represents only one strand of Linguistics. To take an example from a different cultural tradition, language study in India can be traced back as far as the fourth century BC, where scholars such as Panini undertook what we might now call a grammatical analysis – in this case, of Sanskrit (see Katre 1987). The aim of such early studies of language was often to interpret religious texts; there were similar early traditions in China and parts of the Middle East.

In the UK, there had been various kinds of analyses of language well before de Saussure – for example, the tradition of philology, mentioned earlier, which drew on linguistic as well as literary scholarship. However, one reason why de Saussure is marked out as initiating a distinctive approach is that he focused on contemporary usage (termed **synchronic** usage) as well as historical, or **diachronic**, perspectives, seeing linguistic elements as existing in a network of structural relationships. Also, he distinguished language as a system (*la langue*) from language in use (*la parole*). The idea of looking at the language actually used by speakers – as opposed to the language they are thought to use, or the language seen as appropriate for them – is something which characterises English Language study today.

In the USA, early accounts of language-in-use tended to come from researchers with **anthropological** interests. For example, Edward Sapir (1885–1939) and Benjamin Lee Whorf (1897–1941) studied Native American languages and explored the relationship between language, thought and behaviour, raising questions about the extent to which language users could express ideas that were not already encoded in the language they acquired. The idea that language could act as a filter, shaping how speakers see the world, came to be called the **Sapir–Whorf Hypothesis** after these two scholars. More recently, this **deterministic** idea has been challenged and currently a more **relativist** approach is accepted, where language is thought to have a powerful influence but not a totally imprisoning effect.

Although early American Linguistics was quite heavily influenced by the Saussurean tradition, the late twentieth century saw the subject area take a strong **cognitive** direction – that is, a focus on how language is processed by individuals – under the lead of Noam Chomsky. This more psychological orientation, coupled with a focus on whether all languages have an underlying universal similarity in their structure, meant that Linguistics often had a strong presence alongside foreign language learning and teaching in many university departments, including TESOL (the teaching of English to speakers of other languages).

The account above is necessarily brief, and more will be said about the different areas of study in the chapters that follow. However, it is important to note at this point that, unlike the study of literary texts, language work has varied in terms of whether it is seen primarily as an arts and humanities, or a science, subject, and this has influenced where it is housed in universities at a local level. So, while the study of literature is fairly consistently seen as an arts-oriented activity, language study can certainly be oriented towards the arts – for example, studying linguistic patterns in graffiti might well involve thinking about artistic creativity – but it can also be connected with scientific approaches, such as in **speech and language therapy, artificial intelligence** or **forensics**. This breadth is a particular strength of modern approaches to English Language: for example, see the range of applications in Hall *et al.* (2011). However, such variation, along with local specialisms, also means that applicants to courses need to look in some detail at what type of study is being offered, to make sure that it suits individual needs and aspirations.

3

UK 2011 benchmarks for the study of English Language

The Quality Assurance Agency for Higher Education in the UK (QAA) is responsible for ensuring that higher education institutions (HEIs) conform to agreed standards on their programmes, including the scope of different subject areas. The QAA produces statements called 'benchmarks' which describe the nature of academic subjects, including likely subject content, approaches to assessment, and connections to other academic areas.

Benchmarks for English Literature and for Linguistics have existed for some time, but newly growing domains, such as Creative Writing and English Language, have not had their own benchmarks until now. The QAA stopped officially commissioning new sets of benchmarks some time ago, but have supported the production of benchmarks by expert groups, for new subject areas. The benchmark statements for English Language, which are referred to regularly in this book, have this status of guidance.

The benchmark documents are very lengthy and detailed, so are not reproduced here in full: links to them can be found in the References. However, a summary of the most important points for English Language is given below.

The introductory section of the English Language benchmarks notes that a number of different groups will benefit from an outline of the English Language subject area: school teachers who advise school-leavers on the choice of university degree courses; academics considering the introduction of a new degree in English Language, or revalidating an existing one; and employers who wish to understand an applicant's programme of English Language study in greater detail. An obvious audience – perhaps too obvious to mention – are the applicants to university themselves. For that group, the benchmarks are a way of understanding both what an English Language degree might cover, and also how this might vary according to the nature of the university and/or the expertise of the staff group operating the programme. Matching the benchmark statements against modules and/or the staff profiles for a particular course is a useful strategy for understanding what's on offer. The statements – for any subject, not just English Language – are also a good starting point for building up a detailed record of graduate skills for CV purposes. Both future and current undergraduates can make use of the information in Chapter 11, to help build an account of the knowledge and skills that are being developed by their programme.

The benchmark statements below may well contain terms that are unfamiliar. The aim of the chapters that follow is to explain in some detail what the different terms refer to.

Benchmark statements

The nature and scope of the subject

The benchmark statements acknowledge that English Language degrees will vary but stipulate that there should be some common ground consisting of:

- awareness of the structure and use of geographical, social, and historical varieties of English;
- skills shared with General Linguistics in data collection and analysis;
- critical skills shared with Literature, Media Studies, and Anthropology in how discourses represent the world around us;
- awareness shared with Creative Writing courses of the implications of language choices and of the cultural, literary, and historical context in which the texts were produced.

Course coverage

According to the benchmarks, UK degree programmes with 'English Language' in their title are expected to produce graduates who have some awareness of:

- structural aspects of contemporary English;
- approaches to analysing text and discourse;

- how meanings are negotiated between communicators;
- historical, geographical, and social variations in English;
- how English might be compared with other languages;
- issues of language and identity;
- aspects of language and culture;
- the way language choices construct different genres, registers, and styles;
- human language as a communication system in its broadest sense;
- how language analyses can be applied in real-world contexts, such as education, business, the law, performance arts, intercultural negotiations, politics, and the media.

Analytical techniques

The skills developed on an English Language degree include the ability to do the following:

- study samples of text in terms of analytical frameworks ranging from segmental phonetics to the structure and nature of discourses;
- evaluate texts in relation to their purposes and uses, including literary, communicative, sociological, and ideological evaluations;
- analyse underlying language systems at all levels of language, from phonetic to semantic.

Those skills most closely associated with the subject also include:

- critical skills in the close reading, description, analysis, or production of texts or discourses;
- responsiveness to the central role of language in the creation of meaning and a sensitivity to the affective power of language;
- awareness of the variety of Englishes in the world and intercultural awareness.

Although the benchmark statements for English Language have much in common with Linguistics, you will have noticed that they also mention other subject areas, such as Literature, Media Studies, and Anthropology, as well as Creative Writing, from which they also take some approaches.

It is difficult to identify in absolute terms what the difference is between programmes in English Language and those in Linguistics, and this is not spelt out explicitly in the benchmark statements. However, there are general tendencies that can be observed, both in the benchmarks and in other research papers (see Goddard and Beard 2007; Baxter 2009):

- English Language is highly applied, which means that the focus is on how language works in real-world contexts.
- The subject of study is English, which does not rule out looking at different languages, but that is not the primary focus.
- English Language courses are interested in how texts and discourses work, so there may be more emphasis on longer stretches of language and less on single sounds or structures.
- English Language courses are interested not just in how people use language but in what they think about it as well – in order words, in public attitudes and values.
- Although English Language courses are not primarily about communication skills, the expectation is that studying language will enhance learners' ability to use language. Some courses include workplace applications, where students study language use in particular professions.
- An interest in English Language as an academic subject area has coincided with a huge expansion in the use of English as a global language, and the development of new varieties in technologically mediated contexts such as social media. These areas represent potential new applications for applied English Language studies, and explicitly feature on some programmes.

4

Areas of Linguistics

The distinctions drawn at the end of chapter 3 should not be taken to mean that English Language is a completely different subject from Linguistics, because the two fields have much in common. Linguistics remains a strong influence on English Language studies and so this chapter sketches in some background to the different fields of Linguistics that have developed since the inception of the subject at higher education level.

Two very large areas of Linguistics have developed at the interface between language and the social sciences: Sociolinguistics, which connects Linguistics with Sociology (and with Anthropology, which is closely connected with Sociology); and Psycholinguistics, which connects Linguistics with Psychology.

Each of these areas is very wide-ranging, so what you will read about them is necessarily selective. Language and Society, the next section, focuses on ideas about language and social groups, particularly ideas about variation, history, and the politics of language use.

Benchmark statements

The following statements refer particularly to aspects of language and society:

The nature and scope of the subject

- awareness of the structure and use of geographical, social, and historical varieties of English.

Course coverage

- historical, geographical, and social variations in English.

Subject skills

- awareness of the variety of Englishes in the world and intercultural awareness.

Language and society

Language variation

As Sociology is the study of society, it makes sense that Sociolinguistics would focus on the relationship between language and social behaviour. A strong element of Sociolinguistics has been that of **variation**, where studies have attempted to describe how particular groups might differ from each other and from notions of a 'norm'. An influential figure in this field was William Labov, whose studies of accent variation in New York showed that social identity, particularly in terms of the groups that individuals felt affiliated to or aspired to join, was a factor in determining how they pronounced particular sounds (Labov 1966). Labov's work showed how small, apparently insignificant language items could act as a **shibboleth** or 'test word' both to allow some individuals group membership, and to bar others. His work also challenged ideas about how non-standard varieties of language should be viewed – specifically, about the nature of Black English (Labov 1972). He showed that although some aspects of the language of the Black speakers he interviewed varied from standard English, their language was systematic and logical, so there was no basis for calling it 'wrong' or 'mistaken'. As a researcher of language and social behaviour, Labov also revealed some of the processes of language change, as different groups adopt new norms of usage or resist change as a symbolic statement of their social allegiances.

Early Sociolinguistics took on the categories which had been devised in Sociology to represent large-scale social groupings – for example, social class, gender, age, region, occupation, and ethnicity – asking how membership of these social groupings determined an individual's language use. Over time, such clear-cut and rather deterministic ideas about language and social identities have been challenged, particularly the notion that an individual's group membership determines their language use. The idea now would be that language use creates an identity, not the other way round. More will be said about this in Chapter 5.

One example of a departure from the classifications described above is Social Network Theory, used, for example, by Milroy (1987) in studying the strength of people's accents in Northern Ireland. Milroy's study showed that accent was powerfully shaped by how strongly people were tied to the different communities they inhabited, not whether they were male or female, or a member of other large-scale social categories. So rather than, say, gender or age being seen as the reason for particular linguistic realisations, it was social connection or isolation which were important factors. Patterns of connection or isolation could, of course, result from social norms and expectations – for example, the expectation that men would go out to work, and that women would stay at home to look after children. But that's a different perspective from saying that simply being male or female (or old or young, etc.) might trigger differences of language use.

Studies of variation are not the only type of Sociolinguistics it is possible to do. Another aspect, termed **Interactional Sociolinguistics**, focuses less on large-scale variation and more on micro-level individual interactions. Influential figures in this field include John Gumperz (1982), whose starting point was researching how people in interactions use language to achieve **intersubjectivity** – shared understanding, or an attunement to the other's position. His view was that language researchers too often assumed that people in conversations understood each other and shared a common reality, when behind the surface of the words themselves, speakers might have very different understandings of what is being said and how people are behaving. Gumperz' research highlighted the processes of **inference** or assumption that are at work in the moment-by-moment exchanges that we engage in on a daily basis. He and others working in the same field have often applied the study of these processes to the issue of cross-cultural miscommunication, focusing, for example, on how groups can be disadvantaged by not understanding the cultural assumptions behind language use, or stereotyped by others on the basis of their language choices. In powerful institutional contexts such as job interviews, courtroom hearings, and business meetings, miscommunication can have extremely serious consequences.

Another significant figure in Interactional Sociolinguistics was Erving Goffman, whose early work in anthropology is particularly connected with notions of **identity construction**. Goffman's starting point was to see individual identity as a performance akin to that of a character in a drama, and the idea of 'what a person is like' as derived from how we repeatedly perform a consistent kind of persona, giving an illusion of a 'self'. Interestingly, we often use **dramaturgical** vocabulary when we refer to ourselves in everyday talk: for example, we talk about ourselves as having certain traits of 'character', behaving in ways that are 'out of character', filling certain 'roles', being 'upstaged' by others, 'losing the plot', and so on. Even the word 'persona', used above, originally meant a dramatic mask (in Greek tragedy).

At one point, Goffman refers specifically to the well-known Shakespearean metaphor that 'all the world's a stage' and, in a playful twist, takes this at face value:

> Ordinary social intercourse is itself put together as a scene, by the exchange of dramatically inflated actions, counteractions, and terminating replies. Scripts even in the hands of unpractised players can come to life because life itself is a dramatically enacted thing. All the world is not, of course, a stage, but the crucial ways in which it isn't are not easy to specify.
>
> (Goffman, 1969: 62–3)

The idea of identity as a performance continues to have a powerful resonance many years after Goffman's original description in 1959, and to feature in many more subject areas than just English Language or Linguistics. However, these subject areas do owe Goffman a particular debt in that many of his ideas have helped shape language-based approaches to **discourse analysis**, or the study of whole texts or interactions. For example, Goffman elaborated ideas about the different kinds of participation status that an individual might have in an interaction – such as co-participant, animator (someone voicing another person's words), audience member, or bystander – and that each role would entail a different kind of linguistic behaviour within an 'interaction order'. He recognised that participants co-create different types of discourse, dependent on the nature of the activity they are engaged in, and called these different discourses **frames** (Goffman 1974). He also recognised that performance requires not just verbal language use, but, in keeping with the idea of putting on a play of one's own identity, particular 'props' and accessories: for example, the white coats of the medical profession, the gowns and wigs of the law courts, the particular fashions associated with being a student at any one time. An earlier sociologist, Harold Garfinkel, also explored ways in which people come to understand and operate the unspoken social rules within a culture, including how those rules were embedded in conversational exchanges.

A particular field of spoken discourse analysis, **conversation analysis**, has grown out of this interest and, pioneered by the sociologist Harvey Sacks in the 1970s (see the edited volumes in 1995), seeks to understand some of the conversationally based routines behind interactions. A slight difficulty with the name of this field is that it does not cover a wide range of approaches to analysing conversations, but is quite a specific method.

All the theorists, approaches and concepts mentioned above share a common general philosophy, which is to see what we might call 'reality' as socially constructed. This means that what we perceive is not simply given to us but is created by us, and often in ways that are hidden from view because they seem so natural. **Social constructivist** perspectives are certainly not unique to English Language or Linguistics, and there are areas where some linguists would probably not share this perspective: for example, some psycholinguists might want to credit biological factors with more influence. However, academics working within Interactional Sociolinguistics, which has been the focus of this section, are likely to have the kind of view expressed below, by Berger and Luckmann, two early proponents of social constructionism: 'Most conversation does not in so many words define the nature of the world. Rather, it takes place against the background of a world that is silently taken for granted' (1966: 172–3).

Language history

While studies of social variation of language may place more emphasis on looking across a culture or society, studies of language history may well, for obvious reasons, look back in time, sometimes quite extensively. But it is a mistake to think of these two dimensions of synchronic (contemporary) and diachronic (historical) perspectives as unrelated. For example, studies of Old or Middle English can often show how waves of migration or conquest by different cultural groups have formed the basis for differences between English regional dialects in the UK. There are also often differences between the **connotations** of words and phrases that have been absorbed into English from different languages, producing different levels of **formality** in texts or distinctive **registers**. For example, words of Latin or French origin can often produce more formal styles than their Anglo-Saxon (Old English) equivalents; and Latin- and Greek-based terms are frequently used in scientific discourses, particularly in medicine.

Formality is quite a complex concept so it is useful to illustrate the idea with some examples. The examples will also help you to imagine the kinds of

Table 4.1 **Synonyms**

Anglo-Saxon/Scandinavian Languages	French/Latin
snag	impediment
meeting	rendezvous
hairdo	coiffure
clothes	attire
underwear	lingerie

practical activities you might be engaged in on an English Language course. Table 4.1 shows some **synonyms,** with the term on the left derived from old English or Scandinavian languages, while the term on the right is from French or Latin. You can probably see very quickly that although technically the terms are describing similar things, they come from very different contexts of use and suggest different levels of formality as a result. So, for example, you might talk about an 'impediment' to your learning when with teachers and parents at a college open evening, but a 'snag' when talking to your friends about a social arrangement. If you want to critique the idea of synonymy further, you could argue that because of their powerfully different contexts of use and associations, the terms produce very different mental images and so do not 'mean' the same at all. For example, a 'hairdo' might suggest something much more functional than the elaborate style conjured up by 'coiffure'; similarly, 'clothes' might suggest a functional approach to covering your body while 'attire' might sound more like fashion or dressing up for a special event. While 'underwear' might cover both male and female bodies, 'lingerie' is female apparel. And while you might call your college open evening a 'meeting', a college 'rendezvous' sounds more like a romantic tryst than a discussion of job prospects.

My account of what the words in Table 4.1 mean has been tentative, because it is impossible to pin down meaning exactly. When we talk about 'contexts of use' we are assuming that there is a shared understanding of when, where and how certain terms are used within society. Because everyone's experience is different and they will bring their experience to their interpretation of language items, perceptions will vary as will individual **repertoires** of available terms. People within different age groups using **slang** or regional groups using **dialect** might have different repertoires of terms and different perceptions of relative formality. For example, 'clobber' for 'clothes' is a very informal option for some speakers but not for others.

Linguistic enquiry is all about finding evidence of what might start with your own intuitions as a language user. For example, here is a nice example of the use of 'attire', from a Wikipedia contributor describing two styles of 'guernsey' sweater. Note how the writer associates 'attire' with the more formal and upmarket version of the clothing: 'Two styles of guernsey exist: a plain "working" guernsey and a "finer" example that was generally saved for special occasions and Sunday-best attire.' http://en.wikipedia.org/wiki/ Guernsey_(clothing)

One way to get more of an overview of contexts of use is to refer to a **corpus** of language, an electronic database where millions of usages of a term can be collected and then reviewed. A read-out of results called a **concordance** allows a researcher to view a term alongside the other parts of the sentence or utterance that occurred around it. Although language corpora need to be treated with caution as they still represent the language of only some speakers and not everyone, they do offer a little more evidence than a single example or an individual's intuition about patterns of usage. More will be said about corpus methods in Chapter 9.

Tracing back the roots of different words and phrases is called **etymology.** Tracing derivations may appear to be a rather dry activity, but researching borrowings and language change can offer some fascinating insights into cultural influences, including the effects of conquest and colonisation. For example, the suave connotations of the French-based terms for dress and hairstyle above are not accidental. Since the time of the French conquest of Britain in 1066, when French aristocracy took over the key roles in British society, France has been associated with refinement and 'high living'. This is indicated in many other **lexical** domains: for example, cookery, where the French term 'cuisine' suggests fine dining; and manners, where there are many French-derived terms in English for nuances of behaviour and style, such as 'sangfroid', 'savoir faire', 'panache' and 'chic'. Think of the many top-class cosmetics companies and products with French-sounding names – for example, L'Oréal, Laboratoires Garniers, Givenchy, Cacharel – adding to the representation of French culture as highly sophisticated and also romantic.

Lexical items with different derivations can therefore suggest very different profiles or **representations** of cultural groups. This shows how language history connects strongly with modern-day interpretations and is not just about the past. The texts below offer some practical examples of how stylistic choices are connected with our evaluations of different cultural groups. They show how the two sociolinguistic strands of variation and change are inextricably connected.

The box below contains three versions of the same story. They are fictional, playful narratives written by a group of school teachers who were planning ways to help their pupils understand different styles of English (Goddard 2000: 22):

1 Passage 1 is the group's attempt to use the dialect forms of their local region, which was the greater Manchester area.
2 Passage 2 is the group's attempt to 'translate' this into everyday standard English.
3 Passage 3 is the group's attempt to write in as formal a style as possible.

Because the accounts are in the form of anecdotal narratives, they work best if you can read them aloud. But you will still be able to notice plenty of stylistic detail if you are simply reading silently.

As you read through the passages, think about the scenes that you picture from each of the narratives. Are they different in any way? What about the 'voices' that you either feel you need to adopt (if you are reading aloud) or that you hear in your head, as you read silently? For this question, you might think about not just the characters in the story, but also the voice of the **narrator** who is relating the story.

Because the group started with the idea of a local scene, they named the characters in the story in a certain way, and these names have been kept for each of the versions. How do you think the characters' names influence your imaginative construction of the scenes depicted?

If you are from a region of the UK that has a noticeable dialect, try writing your own version of the regional account. If you are using English as your second language, or know other languages, think about whether there are similar stylistic options in those varieties, where one choice would produce much more formality than another.

Different styles of English

Passage 1: The Barney

T'other day, there were a barney at paper shop between Mr Arnold Higginbottom and Mrs. Nora Grimshaw. Mr. Higginbottom had been chunnerin' on about Mrs. Grimshaw's two kids who'd been playing footy in the entry and gawping over his fence when they lost their ball.

Anyroad, Mrs. Grimshaw were gobsmacked about this. She said 'What ya' mitherin' about, ya' lemon? Why are ya' gettin' so nowty?' He said he'd just legged it back from t'factory and he were feeling dead powfagged and he were pig sick of them moping about his yard. He said she should of leathered 'em in't first place and she'd better tell them if they did it again they'd get done.

She said that if it came to complaints, she had a few of her own. His moggy had been messing in her spud patch and had been scratting around there for weeks.

He told her to put a sock in it, and upped and went out of the shop. He barged into an old bid what were trying to come in, knocked his hat off of his head and shoved him to the ground. The old codger started whingeing straight away and were carried off to the hospital where they give him a full check-up. He were shook up and flapping, but apart from a sore lug'ole he were sorted, so they give him a brew and sent him off home for a kip.

Passage 2: The Argument

The other day, there was an argument at the newsagent's between Mr Arnold Higginbottom and Mrs. Nora Grimshaw. Mr. Higginbottom had been complaining about Mrs. Grimshaw's two children who had been playing football in the alleyway and staring over his fence when they lost their ball.

Anyway, Mrs. Grimshaw was surprised about this. She said, 'What are you complaining about, you silly man? Why are you getting so cross?' He said he had just hurried back from the factory and he was feeling really tired and he was fed up with them hanging around in his yard. He said she should have smacked them in the first place and she had better tell them that if they did it again, they would be punished by him.

She said that if it came to complaints, she had a few of her own. His cat had been digging in her potato patch and had been scratching around there for weeks.

He told her to be quiet and left the shop. He bumped into an old man who was trying to come in, knocked his hat off his head and pushed him to the ground. The old man started complaining at once, and was taken to the hospital where they gave him a full check-up. He was very shaken and flustered, but apart from a sore ear, he was all right, so he was given a cup of tea and sent home for a nap.

Passage 3: The Altercation

Recently, there was a fracas at the newsagent's between Mr Arnold Higginbottom and Mrs. Nora Grimshaw. Mr. Higginbottom had been levelling accusations about Mrs. Grimshaw's two offspring who had been engaged in certain team games in the communal passageway and looking fixedly over his fence when they mislaid their ball.

Notwithstanding, Mrs. Grimshaw was absolutely incredulous at this. She said, 'What is the basis of your grievance, you asinine nincompoop? Why are you becoming so irate?' He responded by stating that he had just returned post-haste from the manufacturing establishment and he was feeling utterly fatigued and he was extremely disgruntled to find them loitering on his property. He said that she should have thoroughly reprimanded them at the outset and he would be obliged if she would communicate the fact that if they persisted in their activities, they would be chastised by him.

Her riposte on the subject of grievances was that, in point of fact, she had a number of objections herself. His feline companion had been unearthing her King Edwards and had been disturbing the terrain for some time.

He asked her to desist and made his departure from the premises. He collided with an elderly citizen who was attempting to enter, causing his millinery to be dislodged and jostling him to the ground. The old gentleman expostulated immediately and was accompanied to the infirmary where a thorough examination was conducted upon him. He was extremely tremulous and palpitating, but aside from an injured auditory organ, he was in a satisfactory condition, so he was offered a hot beverage and was despatched homewards to rest and recuperate.

When you look in more detail at the vocabulary of these three passages, you will see that a distinguishing feature of the third passage is its high incidence of Latin or French-based lexis. It may be that you even failed to recognise some of the words, as they are not part of everyday English discourse. If you want to investigate this in more detail, find an etymological dictionary and look up some of the words in the passages. You could locate some of the synonyms (for example, powfagged, tired, fatigued) and research their derivations, but note that if a term is from a regional dialect, it is unlikely you will find it in a mainstream dictionary. This issue is discussed further below.

The politics of language

Although it may not be immediately apparent, the texts you have been reading and thinking about are very revealing of the politics of language use. This does not refer to parliamentary politics, but to politics in the sense of how people are valued and who has access to power and resources within society. The sociologist Bourdieu (1991) termed language a form of **symbolic** power, or capital, where language acts like a kind of currency for individuals to acquire status and privilege (and, conversely, where those in power can decide whose language has the strongest currency).

Exploring the history of language **standardisation** and the idea of official varieties of language (or, in multilingual societies, official languages) is a whole area in its own right. The fact is that standard languages do not become officially sanctioned because they are intrinsically better forms of language, but because they are associated with powerful groups; and studying the history of a language means automatically studying the history of the different groups within the culture.

Standard English was originally the dialect of the South-East Midlands area, and became an official variety because of its proximity to London. If the capital of the UK had grown up around Newcastle upon Tyne, the Geordie dialect would have been chosen as standard English. You will have noticed that the standard English Passage 2 – 'The Argument' – contains some grammatical constructions that are different from many regional varieties, in the form of the verb 'to be'. This is because in the dialect that gave rise to standard English, the past tense of that verb had 'was' in the **singular** and 'were' in the **plural**. Contrast this with, in Passage 1, the regional dialect grammar 'there were a barney' and 'he were', used for singular **subjects**. From a purely linguistic point of view, there is nothing wrong with the language of Passage 1; and yet people are likely to think that both the narrator of the story and the people featured in it were uneducated, and to stereotype them as rough, working-class speakers. There are many other features of the regional passage that might be seen as errors, rather than just as a variety: for example, 'should of' (standard English (SE) 'should have'), 'off of' (SE 'off'), 'what were' (SE 'who was'), 'give' (SE 'gave').

At the other extreme, Passage 3 contains some language that many native speakers of English could probably go a lifetime without needing, for example, 'notwithstanding', 'millinery', 'expostulate', 'tremulous'. Using this highly formal style to describe a silly disagreement between neighbours makes the language seem overblown and comical. And yet, formal language of this kind features in many contexts where important aspects of our lives are being decided – for example, in legal contracts and institutional policies, as well as in medical and scientific documents – and for us not to understand these **discourses** is problematic (see Reeves 2005, on the language of science). Here is a practical example: below is the name of a medical condition, first given its official label, then 'translated' into everyday English. You might consider whether these versions even sound like the same ailment, and whether one version sounds more serious than the other:

benign	paroxysmal	positional	vertigo
harmless	episodes	when in certain positions	of dizziness

There are further contexts you could think about where having limited access to formal styles of English might be disadvantageous. One which is highly relevant to readers of this book is that of academic discourse. There are many different aspects of language that can be covered by the label 'academic', but one area shared by different subject areas is the use of Latin and Greek items, sometimes in their original form. For example, here are some Latin terms that can occur (some quite frequently) in academic writing. If you are interested in exploring this dimension of English discourse, you could find definitions for any terms you are unfamiliar with, then add further terms to the list as you come across them.

ad hoc	ab initio	ipso facto
quid pro quo	inter alia	in medias res
post hoc	et al	de facto
sine qua non	modus operandi	ad infinitum
ad hominem	mutatis mutandis	in camera
tabula rasa	in loco parentis	ex gratia
per se	e.g.	n.b.
etc.	i.e.	ibid
op. cit	sic	viz
curriculum vitae		

So far, discussion of the politics of language has focused on the question of English in the UK. Even if they do not address the question of language politics directly, courses on the history of English will help you to understand the cultural contexts – both collaboration and conquest – that gave rise to the many terms from foreign languages embedded in English.

But there are also contemporary questions to explore about the politics of English world-wide. And here, the idea of variation is not just about different styles of English, but different 'Englishes' altogether. **World Englishes** as a topic area, focuses on understanding both the cultural history and variety of the different Englishes that are used around the world. That is to say, 'native speaker' English is just a small part of the story, as in some post-colonial cultures English might still feature, and be viewed by the resident population in a number of different ways: for example, as an oppressive reminder of former colonisation, as a useful additional language that does not 'belong' to any competing internal group, or as a bit of both.

There are also research questions about how the former colonisers view the new varieties of English that have developed: are they seen as refreshing and interesting new types of English suited to local contexts, or examples of mistaken, badly learned English that are corrupting the original language?

You might think that such issues are a uniquely modern aspect of the World Englishes topic, but people in the UK still periodically express forceful views about American English, although the USA stopped being a British colony in 1776. However, trying to work out who-genuinely-thinks-what in debates about language use in modern times is a rather complex business, as the example below will show.

The complexity of how issues of language are debated and represented is illustrated by an article that appeared in the BBC News Magazine (an online publication) in 2011. The article was entitled 'Viewpoint: Why do some Americanisms irritate people?' and was clearly aiming to be controversial; for example, there is an assumption in the title that people *are* irritated. The writer of the article is not named but its content was based on a talk for Radio 4 given by the journalist Matthew Engel. The written article was therefore a heavily edited version of a previously spoken opinion piece which had been 15 minutes long. In the much reduced written account, what comes across quite forcefully is the **metaphor** of invasion and of being 'taken over'. Here is an extract:

Viewpoint: Why do some Americanisms irritate people?

According to the Oxford Guide to World English, 'American English has a global role at the beginning of the 21st Century comparable to that of British English at the start of the 20th.'

The alarming part is that this is starting to show in the language we speak in Britain. American usages no longer swim to our shores as single spies ... They come in battalions.

American culture is ubiquitous in Britain on TV and the web. As our computers talk to us in American, I keep having to agree to a license spelt with an s. I am invited to print something in color without the u. I am told 'you ghat mail'. It is, of course, always e-mail – never our own more natural usage, e-post.

http://www.bbc.co.uk/news/14130942

As a result of the article, the website received thousands of emails from UK readers, and went on to publish a list of the '50 most noted examples'. Respondents' objections to what they saw as changes to British English were wide-ranging, including one person who said he felt 'disgusted' by his own use of the term 'shopping cart' instead of 'shopping trolley'. But as well as comments from people who seemed genuinely annoyed and upset, there were many contributions that could be read as ironic, in that they appeared to be staging witty performances of outrage and righteous indignation.

It is difficult to work out how seriously we should take the different views expressed by respondents to an online stimulus such as the one described above. This is because an important function of an online media outlet is to generate public response and to entertain, not search for academic truth. And for people who do not share the views of the emailers, the mails offer an entertaining read in themselves. So to some extent, the entertainment factor eclipses other considerations.

But some of the language used in the written article is interesting from an academic point of view. The article sets up a particular attitude by suggesting that American English is 'taking over' in a kind of reverse colonisation. The idea of being taken over makes a connection between issues of language and cultural identities. Strong emotions can come into play when language is being debated because language represents so much more than just a system of communication: it symbolises group membership, with all the ideas of shared values, common feelings and understandings that are entailed.

Perhaps the article provoked a particularly strong reaction in current times because of the rapid development of English as an international language, bringing with it new notions of competition about whose English has the right to be a global **lingua franca**.

For some time, linguists have recognised that there are many more interactions in English involving people speaking English as their second or third language than their first (Graddol 2006). This means that native speakers have a lot of learning to do in order to understand new versions of what was 'their' language, and need to be ready to accept new challenges and new norms of usage.

It is probably no accident that the examples of linguistic colonisation in the article come from the context of new communication technologies. The development of Web 2.0, where users create their own content rather than being passive readers of ready-made sites, has meant that there is more exposure of, and to, English used as a lingua franca. In addition, of course, the global companies manufacturing computer software have up to now been American, so much of the language environment of computer-mediated communication is based on American English, for example, 'trash' and 'mail' (but did British speakers really ever use 'e-post?').

Forms of digital communication are clearly an important aspect of language change both in terms of language features and language practices, and both these areas are ripe for research into how people behave. You might think this is a long way from the politics of language use, but you only have to think about the issues surrounding the items below (see Goddard and Geesin 2011) to realise that in new communication contexts, language is centre stage because it is intimately connected with how we relate to others, construct forms of knowledge and identity, develop ethics, and assert power:

freedom of speech	social networking	online identity
cyberbullying	online advertising	Wikipedia
new literacy skills	online dating	virtual worlds
e-learning	privacy and surveillance	txting
Twitter		

The phenomena of English as a lingua franca (ELF) and computer-mediated communication (CMC) are both in play when we are communicating online with people from different cultures, in the medium of English. While international users of English are evolving their own distinctive forms of ELF, CMC is also generating types of what we might term 'online English' through, for example, needing to write down forms of English that have mainly existed in speech, such as 'OK'.

The chatlog below is from an intercultural chatroom and demonstrates something of the complexities outlined in this section. You can see Dave, a UK student, giving a Swedish student, Helene, some advice on how to spell 'OK'. But, as a highly advanced student of English as a second language, she feels confident enough to challenge this native speaker's knowledge:

Dave: By the way, It might be best to say 'okay' rather than okey.
Helene: Okey!
Dave: Sorry and all that!!!
Helene: Okey! :)

(Goddard 2011)

Although this section has ranged quite widely, the focus has mainly been on written forms of English. The chatlog data might be called 'chat', but the skill involved is a literacy skill because it is about a representation of speech in writing. And the **prescriptive** attitudes both to non-standard English and to new forms of English in CMC contexts tend to revolve around the supposedly 'corrupting' influences at work on standard English. In fact, standard English as a label tends to refer only to written language, and some linguists have charted how the whole idea of standard English came into being, historically (for example, Crowley 2003).

But there are also issues of language politics in the broadest sense that relate to accent and spoken language, rather than to writing. People will readily tell you which accent they like best (including foreign accented English) and which they can't stand hearing, showing, as we have already seen with American English, that we not only use language but have strong attitudes towards it. Sometimes people profess to dislike their own accents, showing that language is linked in our minds with our own concepts of 'self'.

Mapping different UK accents and dialects to show where they occur and how certain features of language are distributed would fall within the domain of Sociolinguistics and be termed **dialectology**. Exploring people's attitudes, and particularly the complex personal reasons for their responses, is normally classified as Social Psychology because it brings together group identities (the 'social' element of the term) with individuals' feelings and judgements (the 'psychological' element of the term).

Language and Social Psychology

Language and Social Psychology focuses on individuals' attitudes to language, trying to uncover their views about the language of particular groups. The best-known studies from the early work in this area are those conducted by Howard Giles and his team (for a useful overview, see Robinson and Giles 2011) on attitudes to accent. They conducted experimental studies where groups of people were asked to listen to different speakers and rate them for various characteristics and dimensions, such as personality traits or markers of status. Giles often used a technique called **matched guise**, where actors assumed a range of accents and pretended to be different speakers. This was in order to rule out the variables that could have arisen from the real differences that exist between speakers. The argument was (and still is, as this type of experiment is still conducted) that if you rule out individual differences by having a single speaker, listeners cannot be responding to anything else in the judgements they make apart from their own evaluations of the accent in question.

There is a general consensus that Britain has a much more tolerant attitude to accent varieties than was the case when the work of social psychologists such as Giles began to be published in the 1970s. At that time, Received Pronunciation, or RP, had high prestige and few public broadcasters had any other kind of accent. Now, a wide variety of speakers are heard, and

phoneticians such as Wells (1982) have charted the rise of a new prestige norm in the form of **Estuary English**. However, there is still no such thing as a 'neutral' or non-existent accent, as all accents will provoke judgements on the part of the listener about the speaker's affiliation to particular groups such as region and social class.

While matched guise accent experiments might work for studies of attitudes to regional forms of language, they would not work in researching the **stereotypes** associated with other social dimensions such as gender, age, or ethnicity, because the capacity of a single speaker to imitate different voices is limited. However, research in social psychology has contributed to our understanding of public attitudes towards language, particularly towards the language of marginalised groups and the idea that their language is somehow to blame for their lack of power. The idea that people in some social groups are held back by their use of language is called a **deficit model** of language use and this idea characterised early research on language and **gender**. We will return to this idea later in this book when we consider issues of social representation.

Of course, **informants** or interviewees do not have to be played examples of language use in order to be asked for their views about the language of particular social groups. Language in one form or another is something that we all share and so everyone will have a reference point for questions that are asked of them. The relationship between an individual's views and the culture they inhabit is at the core of studies of social psychology, so any answer given is revealing.

Labov showed many years ago that individuals' pronunciations of sounds varied according to their social affiliations and aspirations. A further area of Giles' work has been the development of **communication accommodation theory (CAT)**, which focused on the idea of **style shifting** as individuals interact with others who are different in social status. CAT explores the phenomenon of **convergence** and **divergence** in language use, looking at how individuals in conversations move towards or away from the language of their interlocutor (Giles *et al.* 1991). CAT draws on **Social Identity Theory**, showing how the behaviour of individuals connects with their attitudes towards social groups (Tajfel [1982] 2010).

Language and mind

Just as sociolinguistics refers to an inter-relationship between language and society or social groups, so psycholinguistics focuses on the inter-relationship between language and the individual. Sociolinguists are interested in the role that language plays in how we live as social beings; psycholinguists are interested in the psychological processes that underlie our language use. Of course, these aspects are not separate: we function both as individuals and as people with social relationships. More than this, how we think and express ourselves as individuals is likely to help shape our social lives; and conversely, how we participate in society will have an effect on our language and our thinking, particularly on our self-concepts.

The previous section on language and social psychology will have helped you to understand the inter-connectedness of the dimensions described above. The next section will shift the focus again, this time moving more towards psychological aspects in order to consider some aspects of language and the individual.

Benchmark statements

The following statements invite psychological perspectives on language:

Course coverage

- human language as a communication system in its broadest sense;
- how meanings are negotiated between communicators.

The field of Psycholinguistics is very wide, including work on mental representations (how language is stored in the memory), how it is processed (produced and understood), and how it is acquired, including atypical development. On university courses, these areas could be explored via a whole module in each case, sometimes involving very scientific work (for example, language and disability might include aspects of **neurolinguistics**). Because of the wide scope of the area, it is necessary to be selective. Most of the space below is devoted to language and cognition, or thinking processes, as this topic provides an accessible starting point.

Language and thought

In Chapter 2, we saw that in exploring some of the differences between languages, Sapir and Whorf were led to consider whether language shapes our thinking, particularly whether we can ever 'escape' the language we're given as part of the culture that surrounds us as we grow up. Although nowadays it is recognised that we are not entirely imprisoned by language – otherwise we would not be able to think up new terms, and language would never change – work still continues on the relationship between language and thought, because there are still many unanswered questions. But one of the difficulties in researching thought, of course, is that its working is mysterious because it is essentially an invisible process: as people are thinking, we cannot see what is going on inside their brains. And although developments in technology have allowed us more information about brain activity, such as which parts of our brains are active in certain contexts, we still have much to understand about how our mental processes work.

Sociolinguists researching language and thought might look at this relationship in terms of how thoughts are expressions of a society's cultural values, and seek evidence in linguistic outputs such as pieces of writing, speeches, and interactions of all kinds. However, psycholinguists are interested in the thinking processes that underlie expression and that make up the structures that we follow as we exercise our brains on the many aspects of living and communicating that are necessary for human functioning. The nature of these structures, and how they relate to each other, are sometimes referred to as the 'architecture' of cognition. This raises another problem, which is that the way we talk about invisible aspects of ourselves is often metaphorical – in this case, we are construing brains as buildings – so we are back once again to Sapir and Whorf conundrum of how to escape our own language use. As you can see, there are no easy answers in this area of language study but many interesting questions to explore.

It is important to recognise that there are many different ways of approaching the topic of language and thought so it is essential not to have too rigid a set of expectations of what this may cover. For example, it would be possible to debate this area in a very philosophical way, as philosophers from Aristotle to Wittgenstein and beyond have proposed their own views on the nature of human language. Wittgenstein in particular saw a focus on language as essential to his approach to philosophy, which is sometimes called 'linguistic philosophy', or 'ordinary language philosophy' as a result. His work stressed the connection between 'meaning' and contexts of use, articulated here in a quote from his most famous work, the *Tractatus Logico-Philosophicus*: 'The limits of my language mean the limits of my world' (Wittgenstein 1961).

Wittgenstein saw the philosopher's work as making people clarify their thinking by questioning the familiar habits of language use:

Language sets everyone the same traps; it is an immense network of easily accessible wrong turnings. And so we watch one man after another walking down the same paths and we know in advance where he will branch off, where walk straight on without noticing the side turning, etc. etc. What I have to do then is erect signposts at all the junctions where there are wrong turnings so as to help people past the danger points.

(Richter 2004)

Language and cognition

Language and cognition focuses on the role of language in thinking processes, seeing language as an embodied phenomenon – in other words, part of our physical being. In Chapter 2, the American linguist Noam Chomsky was mentioned as an influential figure in the development of cognitive approaches to language study in the latter half of the twentieth century, and although his work was often theoretically based rather than applied, any course in this area is likely to include references to his work. Chomsky maintained that the speed at which humans seemed able to acquire language could not be adequately explained by **behaviourist** approaches, which gave the role of imitation central importance. His explanation of the human facility he observed was that, although language looked impossibly complex to learn at the surface level, there was a set of 'deep structures' or 'rules' which could generate an infinite number of new utterances. These rules were part of the **syntactic** structure of any language and explained why people are able to feel that even nonsense language is interpretable. Chomsky's famous example was: 'Colourless green ideas sleep furiously'.

Chomsky's best-known early work was entitled, unsurprisingly, *Syntactic Structures* (1975). Its interest value to researchers in psychologically oriented fields lay in the fact that Chomsky looked beyond the surface patterns of language and proposed a level of cognitive processing which could recognise deeper connections. So, for example, a pattern which looked the same at a surface level, such as the following:

John is easy to please
John is eager to please

is understood as different because the 'deep structure' is being accessed and connected via systematic transformations with their surface realisations.

Chomsky's influence has been particularly felt in the field of language acquisition. In particular, his work on **generative grammar** has enabled researchers to think about language learners as active processors of language and not simply passive rote-learners. In acquiring language, children can be seen to be learning the structural rules of the language, so many of their mistakes can be viewed as logical – evidence of a rule learnt, rather than some kind of careless error.

Chomsky is also well known for his proposition that humans are predisposed to learn language, calling this supposedly **innate** facility a 'language acquisition device'. There will always be debate about how much of human nature in general is innate and how much is the result of socialisation, but whatever the balance is, the components of human language now tend to be seen, not as unique to language, but as shared with other aspects of human cognitive functioning – such as memory and attention, for example.

One of the benchmark statements listed earlier referred to 'human language as a communication system in its broadest sense', and there are interesting questions to explore about how human language compares with the communication systems of the other living beings that are on the planet. Looking back now, some of the animal experiments that were conducted (not by psycholinguists) in the 1960s and 1970s in order to challenge the idea of the uniqueness of human language now seem very cruel. These activities were exposed in *Project Nim*, a film made in 2011 about the work of Herbert Terrace, who tried to teach a chimp human language (Terrace called his chimp Nim Chimpsky, in a teasing reference to the famous linguist). The film voices harsh criticism of the human motivations and actions in the whole enterprise of training animals to be part of human communities.

Although public attitudes towards animal experimentation are now very different, there is still academic interest in evolutionary questions about how human language – for example, how our brains have evolved to perform particular functions and how human language compares with the communication systems of other species.

Chomsky's own work sought to establish linguistic universals, which meant going beyond particular languages and establishing models and rules that could be applied to all human language. This approach to language study would be termed **theoretical linguistics**, and there are still fields of grammatical analysis that take Chomsky's work further with that view in mind – for example, **x-bar theory**. However, the idea of 'universalism' is much more controversial than in previous years, with **postmodern** approaches in Linguistics and elsewhere challenging the idea of authority that is inherent in such an approach.

Chomsky's theoretical approach can be illustrated by considering the type of language user he had in mind when developing his model. His focus was on the aspect of **competence**, rather than **performance**. Similar to de Saussure's categories of '*la langue*' and '*la parole*' respectively, 'competence' described the idea of the abstract rules we have in our heads about the language system, while 'performance' related to the often imperfect result of our attempts to communicate with others in real life. In his own words, Chomsky's model was based on: 'an ideal speaker-listener in a completely homogeneous speech-community, who knows its language perfectly'. This idealised figure was someone unaffected by such 'grammatically irrelevant' conditions as: 'memory limitations, distractions, shifts of attention or interest, and errors (random or characteristic) in applying his knowledge of the language in actual performance' (Chomsky 1965: 3).

This is a very different starting point from that which would be adopted by, for example, the sociolinguists who describe variation, discussed earlier in this chapter. It would also be different from that of many psycholinguists, and particularly those researching language and cognition, where a focus on 'memory limitations, distractions, shifts of attention …' might be the very phenomena of interest. A focus on language use, and language users, with the aim of shedding some light on issues and problems – what you might see as the 'messy' aspects of real-world language use – characterises much of the work both of sociolinguists and psycholinguists, and would be termed an **applied** approach.

In the area of language and cognition, there are many complex processes to explain even the seemingly very mundane and fleeting acts of communication we engage in every day. Taking just speech, these processes would include speakers turning their thoughts into sounds and hearers translating those sounds into some kind of meaningful message, all at remarkable speed. If you are interested in unpicking some of the aspects that we take for granted and appear to manage so effortlessly – or that, for a variety of reasons, can go wrong and escape our management – then there is a rich field in this area of language study to explore.

Language and iconicity

One area of interest for cognitive linguists is that of iconicity, which is all about the relationship between the ordering and organisation of linguistic elements and our perceptions of the real world. For example, in Julius Caesar's supposed triumphal announcement after a battle in 47 BC – 'Veni, vidi, vici' – which is Latin for 'I came, I saw, I conquered', the ordering of the words suggests the unfolding of these events in time. In the many **intertextual** versions of this phrase that can be found in modern times, that temporal ordering is maintained. For example, here is a chatroom participant on an online university course complaining that he arrived at the allotted time for a group session only to find himself alone:

Glyn: I came, I saw, and nobody turned up.

(Goddard 2005)

Here is a newspaper headline about bird migration:

They came, they soared, they conquered.

(Thynne 2010)

And Figure 4.1 shows a bag for sale in a tourist shop in York, in the UK. (York had extensive Roman settlement, and its Roman name was 'Eboracum'.) Visa, of course, is the name of the card payment system that shoppers often use.

In all these examples, the order of the words is presumed to reflect the order of the actions. This order is so fixed that any reorganisation would be **marked** as different from the norm, and therefore **salient** – understood as needing special attention. This is the case in Figure 4.2, which is a t-shirt slogan but has also occurred as the hookline in a condom ad.

Figure 4.1 Intertextuality for sale: a bag in a shop window

Figure 4.2 **Intertextuality for sale: t-shirts to order**
Source: Reproduced with kind permission of taiche.

The ordering of events is one type of sequential order. But there are other types of sequence that suggest not just ordering through time but a possible order of priority. So, for example, in phrases such as 'he or she', 'husband and wife', 'Mr and Mrs', 'boys and girls', 'men and women', 'male and female', the suggestion would be that the linguistic ordering reflects – and constructs, in our minds – the social importance of the people referred to. This was the claim made by early research on language and gender (Miller and Swift 1980; Spender 1980), leading to much debate and some increased awareness among writers of the implications of their language choices.

Another kind of ordering relates to the position of different **modifiers** around an item, with the modifier that is in closest **proximity** to the central item being seen as the most important. You can see this proximity principle in action in the **phrases** below, taken from *The Sun* newspaper:

personalised greeting card firm MOONPIG (financial news feature)
http://www.thesun.co.uk/sol/homepage/news/money/3714435/
Money-happy-returns.html

famous London restaurant The Ivy (holiday feature)
http://www.thesun.co.uk/sol/homepage/travel/2302776/Holiday-
News-A-British-flavour-at-Butlins.html

high quality self-catering accommodation
Big Green Weekends

(both from travel page, about eco-tourism)
http://www.thesun.co.uk/sol/homepage/
travel/3686561/Holiday-News-Natural-retreats-
in-Yorkshire-Dales.html

Language and categorisation

Much effort has gone into exploring the activity of categorisation, because it is seen as crucial to thinking processes. We are all aware of how children seem relentless gatherers of the names of items and beings around them. What they are doing is learning the way categories work in the culture and the language that surrounds them. This process can be seen in action in children's lexical **overextension**, where they apply a category label they have learned to items that are beyond that category. For example, a child might say 'ball' to any item that is round, including oranges, balloons, and the moon. It is interesting that as adults we often find children's thinking in this way very creative and pleasing. This is often because children have not learned the constraints that, as adults, we routinely follow, and their rule-breaking reminds us that there are other possible ways to draw the boundaries. This is not so different to the qualities we admire in creative writing, which can offer us fresh perceptions of familiar ideas.

Although the categories embedded in our own language feel logical and natural, they are neither clear-cut nor universal. Different languages have different ways of categorising experiences, things, and people. For example, in Dyirbal, an Australian aboriginal language, Lakoff (1987) claims that the category 'balan' includes women, fire, and other 'dangerous things'.

Categories that look very cut and dried are also, on closer scrutiny, more complex than you might think. While it appears on the surface that a category label, such as 'bird', might contain category members that were all equally valid, you may feel that a robin or a sparrow is a more classic example of a bird than, say, a chicken or a penguin. The category member that is seen to have classic qualities – in the case of 'birdiness' this could, for some people, be a combination of features such as flight, size and feathers – is termed a **prototype**.

The existence of prototypes, or classical examples of category membership, indicates that different members are accorded different status. While the

39

importance of that may not seem obvious where a category such as 'bird' is concerned, its application to human groups shows its significance, where we might be thinking that certain qualities are prototypical for, say, the category 'male' or 'female'.

The associations that we attach to terms are called **connotations**, and this aspect of meaning, while not necessarily in the dictionary, is thought to be very powerful. The network of associations that are repeatedly rehearsed in the texts and discourses around us, sets up cultural stereotypes where the qualities of the prototype are expected in all occurrences. For example, it was suggested that we see French culture as chic, sophisticated, and romantic, so do we expect all French people to conform to those ideas? Morgan (1986: 179), investigating gender stereotypes, claims that, through repeated occurrence in everyday texts, males are seen as 'logical, rational, aggressive, exploitative, strategic, independent and competitive', while females are seen as 'intuitive, emotional, submissive, empathic, spontaneous, nurturing and co-operative' (see Goddard and Mean 2009, for discussion).

These ideas can be explored via practical activities on English Language programmes. For example, imagine that you had collected the two images that were used in the previous section (Figures 4.1 and 4.2). You could then explore the abstract categories of 'male' and 'female' by considering how gendered a picture you are offered, of the bag and the T-shirt. Would you expect to see the bag in Figure 4.1 marketed to men? How about the T-shirt in Figure 4.2 – could this be worn by a woman? What characteristics are associated with male and female figures, via these items? Although our thinking may be abstract, we can still see some expression of our categorising processes in tangible outcomes. We can also observe our own thinking processes as we interpret the messages that surround us.

Language and metaphor

Metaphor is an interesting aspect of cognitive activity because it is about departing from the normal connections we might make in our thinking, and putting things together in a new way. As was suggested in the previous section, creating new pathways in our thinking is something that we tend to associate with creative authors; and you might have come across metaphor before if you have studied literature, as that's where discussion of this feature happens regularly in the school system. However, cognitive linguists have researched this aspect of language use for some time, recognising that metaphor is not just confined to novels and poetry but is an everyday feature of language use (Lakoff and Johnson 1980).

In this book, the first mention of metaphor was in the BBC article written by a journalist, where examples of American English were described as a 'battalion'. This is a metaphor because it links together two normally unrelated ideas – language and war – to describe a scenario that cannot be literally true. This particular metaphor may also be referring to an earlier metaphor used by Shakespeare in his play, *Hamlet*, where a character describes sorrows as coming not as 'single spies' but in vast numbers. The linguistic items that are referred to cannot literally be an army coming across from the USA and landing on the shores of Britain. However, using this metaphor allows the journalist to convey a strong message, so there is meaning being created even though the thinking required is not straightforward. One suggestion that has been made about metaphor is that it is often motivated by a writer or speaker wishing to convey strong emotion (Morgan 1986). That certainly seems true in this case.

There are different ways to refer to the component parts of a metaphor. Writing in a more literary tradition, Richards (1936) termed the subject of the metaphor (in this case, American English) the 'topic', and the way it is being described the 'vehicle' (in this case, an army). Lakoff and Johnson (1980), drawing more on cognitive science, use 'target' instead of topic and 'source' instead of vehicle.

However the parts of the expression are described, what is noticeable about the language-as-army metaphor is that, although it is not literally true, the idea fits with other ways that we talk of language and national identity. Language is a strong symbol of cultural identity, and the idea of one group invading another and imposing its language on the vanquished group is familiar to us in countless examples from history. Think, for example, of 1066 and how the French invasion of Britain brought the French-speaking aristocracy to power and relegated English to a street language.

In using the metaphor of language-as-army, then, the BBC journalist is using what is sometimes known as a **conceptual metaphor**: that means that the expression fits in with other types of metaphorical thinking about the subject in question. So if we talk of languages being 'killed off', of 'languages in conflict', of one language 'winning a struggle for survival', we are elaborating similar ideas of language as a living being engaged in battles.

In the case of language-as-army example, there are of course further associations that connect, not just with language, but with ideas of American cultural dominance and contemporary debates about US military involvement in different parts of the world. The article taps into the idea of American military aggression to shore up the argument about the invasive nature of American English. The writer chooses not to mention the much older

English language invasion of America where English 'killed off' its rivals, including many First Nation (American Indian) languages. That case, of course, involved real battalions and the languages were killed because the speakers died.

The example above has been discussed at some length because it's a good example of the way individual thinking and expression are connected with the larger culture that surrounds us. A further example of metaphor – this time a bit more subtle and harder to spot – will focus not on professional writers like journalists but on the everyday language use of ordinary individuals.

The area of computer-mediated communication has seen growing interest from cognitive researchers because of the opportunities it offers to capture participants' behaviour in a new environment. When people are using a new form of communication, it can lay bare some of the thinking processes that more familiar contexts fail to reveal. That is because people are engaged in learning, which often involves making mistakes, testing boundaries, and changing tack as they learn what works and what doesn't. Although many people now find computer-based communication very familiar, there are always new types of communication being developed requiring new learning. Any researcher looking at language acquisition cannot ignore the huge impact new technologies have had on how we learn language.

The computer environment is highly metaphorical in that the names of the various tools are based on their real-world equivalents but are not the same thing. For example, a chatroom is not a room and for the most part involves written text, so cannot really be chat in the literal sense (although some chat tools have voice facility). Files and folders are electronic simulations, as are spaces, which are not three-dimensional in the conventional sense of the word. In other words, all our real-world physical parameters have been reset in virtual space, but, in the interests of marketability, computer software companies need us to feel that we are in familiar territory. We even have culturally sensitive changes to language use as systems are upgraded: for example, what used to be termed the 'trash' or 'wastebasket' is now the 'recycle bin' on many computer desktops – which, of course, are neither desks, nor tops.

One area that refers to how language is embodied in individual perception is that of **indexicality**, which expresses (literally 'points out' like an index finger) where people and things are in the physical world. The data below is from a chatroom on an online university course run in 2000, where the participants were new to each other and also to being online in general. One of the many noticeable aspects of their language use included their immediate use of indexical terms, such as 'in', 'out', 'here', and 'there' to describe their own and others' positions and movements in virtual space, even though these terms did not have physical referents. What you can see in these examples is their creation of the idea of three-dimensional space – the creation of a 'world' – through their use of language. You could therefore describe their deictic expressions as a kind of metaphor.

> The chatlog examples are reproduced exactly as they were written. However, the five lines below have been taken from different parts of the chatlog, so were not a continuous conversation.

> 'is there anyone in here?'
> 'is anyone coming in?'
> 'anyone there?'
> 'is there anybody out there?'
> 'Hello spirits is their any one out there?'

In the exchange below, you can see one of the participants showing they know the language they are using is odd. Al enters the chatroom first, followed by Anne:

> Al: there you are
> Anne: no, I'm not there, I'm here

> (Goddard 2003)

Language and meaning: scripts, schemas and beyond

A further area that may be covered on an English Language programme is that of language and meaning. This section will explore the meaning of 'meaning' by outlining some of the linguistically-oriented approaches that have been taken to it. As you would expect, there is no single or easy definition; and you need to be aware that different academic subject areas may well have quite radically opposing views. This is fine, of course: academic study should be about debate and argument.

The discussion of meaning in Linguistics is often associated with an area called **semantics**, which at a basic level includes the meanings of words, or even parts of words, and their relationship to each other, which is often referred to as **sense relations**. An example of sense relationship is synonymy, and this was discussed in the box on p. 22 in the context of the Barney/ Argument/Altercation passages. However, as you saw there, it is debatable whether these alternative terms really 'mean' the same thing, if meaning includes all their associations and contexts of use. It was suggested earlier that connotation plays a large part in creating meaning, and that some of the principles of lexical organisation we might think are cut and dried are possibly subject to much interpretive variation. The chapter went on to suggest that expressions have connections way beyond their local usage and play a role in the much larger public discourses that you might see as 'conversations' between cultures and across time. Semantics understood simply as 'the meanings of words' can therefore offer some useful starting points for thinking about meaning, but is by no means the end of the story.

Another area of linguistics which attempts to address questions of meaning is **pragmatics**, which focuses less on the language system itself and more on what users do with language. This contrast can be described as a difference between **structural** accounts of language, and **functional** ones.

The terms semantics and pragmatics can be found in texts outside of Linguistics, and in the case of pragmatics, which is not easy to define, its general meaning is a useful guide. To call someone a 'pragmatist' suggests they are flexible and practical, realistic, ready to adapt to new situations as they find them. The term, as used in Linguistics, shares something of that meaning, as the area explores the ways in which we use language according to the context we are in, and how we think we can best express our intended meaning. For example, we may think we need to be indirect in some contexts, in which case our readers or listeners might need to 'read between the lines' of what we say in order to get at what we really mean. Pragmatics, then, looks at the relationship between words, intentions, and understandings.

Because pragmatics tries to explore what is meant and not just what is said, some of its influences have been from writers in philosophical traditions attempting to formulate general principles for understanding meaning. For example, **speech act theory** (Searle 1969) was an early attempt to show how language was a way of doing things in both the everyday sense – for example, promising to meet someone or work to a deadline – as well as in institutional contexts such as courts and religious settings, where we might be swearing an oath to tell the truth or pledging to act in a certain way in future.

Later cognitive approaches, such as Clark and Brennan's (1991) concept of 'grounding' in communication, also called 'common ground' (Clark 1996), focused more on the idea of the mutual knowledge, beliefs and assumptions that were thought to be necessary for people in interactions to understand each other. This does not refer to beliefs in any grand sense, but some mutual commitment that you and your interlocutor share some expectations – for example, that you are both telling the truth, or that you are both engaged in a certain kind of task.

Another cognitive approach, that of **relevance theory** (Sperber and Wilson 1995), explores ideas about the implicit and inferential nature of meaning. These theorists suggest that speakers think their communication is relevant to their hearer's context, preferences and abilities, and that speakers give only the amount of information necessary for their hearers to understand the intention of the communication. At the same time, hearers believe that what they are being told is relevant, and that the communication is worth making the effort to understand. Sperber and Wilson suggest that the number of thoughts we articulate is smaller than the number we think, so that a great deal of work goes into the interpretation of what we choose to communicate, the idea being that communication is meaningful.

A further exploration of the idea of relevance can be seen in theories of **schemas** and **scripts** (Schank and Abelson 1977) which emerged from cognitive psychology and work on artificial intelligence, respectively. These theories suggest that we have ready-made constructs of ideas and associated forms of language use that we can deploy when we encounter known contexts, such as going into a restaurant and ordering dinner, or going to a party, or going to a lecture ... the list is potentially very long.

A quick example can be given here from the same chatlog data source that was used for the examples on p. 43. The discussion of the data earlier focused on the participants' metaphorical use of deictic terms. But you will have noticed that they were also playing with the idea that they were in particular scenes. For example, the line below suggests that the online space is 'out there' in the spirit world, in its echo of the classic 'is there anybody there?' of séances:

Hello spirits is their any one out there?

You could also argue that this line, too, suggests an other-worldliness, this time of the outer space variety:

is there anybody out there?

Other examples from the same chatlog of the creation of particular kinds of spaces include a bar, where two participants square up for a mock-fight:

mr [name omitted] are you threatening me
Yes mr [name omitted] that is exactly what i'm doing
come on you and me outside

a family scene, with scolding parents:

oi clean your room
stop it and tidy up!

and a street encounter with a policeman:

hello hello hello

(Goddard 2005)

In all these examples, the 'scenes' are suggested by a form of scripting of language – we get the kind of language we expect from this context, and are able to then visualise the episode. The example of the pub or bar illustrates the idea of schemas in that a whole schema would involve all the different activities we associate with going to this kind of social space, the punch-up being just one of them.

There are several further terms that could be used to describe the language associated with specific contexts, including register, or **field** (Halliday 2004). We will come back to these ideas shortly, when we think about the nature of discourse.

You can probably already recognise some of the difficulties facing researchers in the field of pragmatics. Some theories can be criticised for focusing simply on the language system, without engaging with real discourse. On the other hand, if pragmatics is all about the context of speakers' communication – their knowledge, circumstances, setting, their past histories, and so on – there is a huge amount of extra information required to study their communication, and some would say this takes research beyond the scope of language study. There are some long-standing fields of research in social science which have explicitly tried to set out all the factors that are part of the communication context – for example, Hymes' (1962) development of a field originally called the 'ethnography of speaking' (later, the ethnography of communication) – but the quantity of information produced is sometimes challenging to manage. How to connect the analysis of individual acts of communication with the larger fabric of their cultural contexts is the subject of ongoing debate in language study. Perhaps you can now see why both sociolinguistic and psycholinguistic approaches can make important contributions to our understanding of language.

The emphasis in the chapters so far has been much more on spoken language than on writing. For example, in considering accent variation and attitudes to language, as well as language acquisition and pragmatics, the default notion of language has been 'talk'.

The focus on speech is not an authorial quirk. The subject area of linguistics grew up around the study of spoken language, and in some universities it is called 'speech science(s)'. **Phonetics** and **phonology** (how sounds are produced and the sound systems of languages) are an important part of linguistic study, and form the basis for clinical applications for health professions such as speech and language therapy. More will be said about the sound system when we discuss metalanguage, in Chapter 7.

Writing does of course feature in research with a language focus: for example, **critical discourse analysis**, which aims to study issues of language and power (see Fairclough 2001) often uses written texts, such as newspaper articles, as data. But this type of discourse analysis has a strong **interdisciplinary** framework, where researchers connect language use with some of the critical questions that are addressed in other subject areas.

Chapters 5 and 6 look at the contribution that ideas from Literary and Media Studies, and Creative Writing, can make to analysing language, particularly written communication. Chapter 7 takes the idea of interdisciplinarity further afield.

5

Areas of Literary and Media Studies

This chapter is not about the overall study of literature or the media, as that would be far too large a scope to attempt here. Rather, it focuses on some of the ideas and concepts that are part of study in those areas. The aim is to show how those ideas can be used in analysing language.

Although this book is not addressing itself specifically to readers who are interested in studying English Literature at higher education level – readers in that position are referred to Robert Eaglestone's (2002) *Doing English*, in this series – there will be some useful insights in the sections that follow on how to take a more language-oriented approach to literary material. The discussion that follows is not about literary authors, or about literary texts, as such. But it is about notions of 'literariness' and about how literary material is constructed. It may be that if your real love is literature, looking at language can make you appreciate its skilful artifice even more.

For students of language, literary and media texts are an obvious source of data for researching how ideas are communicated via language choices. Literature is, after all, made up of language and is a powerful form of communication. For language students, too, there are interesting and relevant questions about 'literariness': language students might use their insights into literary texts to question whether there is any such thing as 'literal meaning', or whether supposed everyday language in fact shares many qualities with literature.

Benchmark statements

The following statements for English Language refer particularly to ideas and activities that are common in the study of English Literature and in Media Studies:

The nature and scope of the subject

- how discourses represent the world around us.

Course coverage

- approaches to analysing text and discourse.

Analytical techniques

- evaluate texts in relation to their purposes and uses, including literary, communicative, sociological, and ideological evaluations

Text, discourse and discourses

The terms text, discourse, and discourses have all been used already in this book, and, in the case of the latter term, have been defined in the glossary. However, it is worth spending a little more time on these terms as they have particular histories, and also slightly different meanings across different subject areas. If and when you encounter these terms on your English Language course, you'll then be able to understand how they are being used.

Text is a common term in **literary criticism** as this has traditionally been the label used for literary works, or the written artefacts that authors produce. Critics and analysts discuss literary texts for many different reasons, but at the core of the term 'text' is the idea of a whole product. A text is seen to have a kind of internal unity, and boundaries defining where it starts and stops. That is not a comment on the way the text is organised or communicates its ideas: for example, readers of James Joyce's *Ulysses*, which uses many different **narrative** devices, may well struggle to piece these different elements of the text together. But that is partly the point of *Ulysses* – to reflect that real life is a lot more multi-layered than the picture we are normally given in novels. But however difficult it might be to read, *Ulysses* is packaged and experienced by readers physically as a whole entity. Even *The Unfortunates*, an experimental novel in loose leaf format where the reader had to assemble the text themselves (Johnson 1999), came in a box.

In Linguistics, text has also tended to refer to writing, and to focus on the idea of material that is seen to have internal connections, or **cohesion**. Halliday and Hasan's (1976) definition of cohesion stresses the way elements of language tie a text together, giving it a holistic feel: 'Cohesion is what gives a text texture.'

Halliday takes a functionalist approach to texts, which means a focus on what the purposes of the text are, trying to identify the cohesive elements of the text that hold it together and make it what it is. However, the sentence that started this paragraph referred to 'material that is *seen to have* internal connections', and this is a crucial factor as far as literary approaches are concerned. A writer might have certain purposes in mind and put a text together using particular language choices which they think will express their meaning; but that is no guarantee that a reader will interpret the text as the writer intended. What a text means, then, is extensively debated within literary criticism, going far beyond simple notions of authorial intention, and sometimes even seeing the whole notion of intention as irrelevant to meaning.

There are of course many different schools of interpretation in literary studies, but an important common idea in recent times is that a reader does not come to a text empty-handed, as it were. Texts are not messages sent from A to B, with the receiver simply being handed a prefabricated meaning. Readers bring all their experiences, expectations, past and current contexts to bear when they interpret a text. This idea is at the core of **reader response theory** (Fish 1980), which stressed the importance of individual perception but also the idea of 'interpretive communities', with their shared assumptions and understandings. The importance of context to the interpretation of text is illustrated in Fish's classic example of a university class who entered their teaching room to find some words written on the board at the front. Fish shows how easily these words were seen as a text, with the class members able to make sense of what were, in effect, completely random words written by another tutor. The point is that although there were no obvious elements of cohesion (to use Halliday's term), the class created some, interpreting the words as a poem.

An important contribution that a literary approach to English Language can make in the study of texts, therefore, is the emphasis on readership and not just authorship.

It is important to recognise that the term 'text' is also used in other academic areas and is not simply confined to English Language or English Literature.

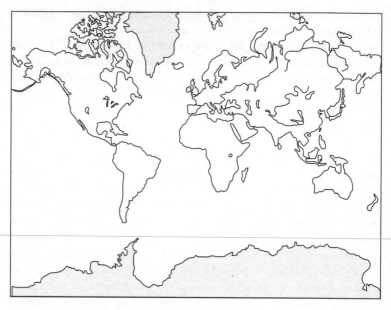

Figure 5.1 The Mercator map

For example, in Anthropology, which is the study of human societies and allied to Sociology, a building can be a text because it can be 'read' or interpreted in a certain way; in Art, a painting can be a text, for the same reason, as can a film in Media Studies; in Geography, maps can be texts because they are representations, to be interpreted. A classic example of the latter is the Peters Projection map (Figure 5.2), which showed an alternative representation of the earth to that of the previous standard map, the Mercator (Figure 5.1). Peters claimed that the Mercator had wrongly represented the relative sizes of countries by inflating those which were furthest away from the Equator. As a result, in the Mercator map, Greenland appears to be a similar size to Africa, when in fact (in terms of ground measurement) Africa is 14 times the size of Greenland. A more accurate representation of the relative sizes of Africa and Greenland can be seen in Figure 5.2, which is drawn to the Peters scale.

How different countries are shown on a map might seem to be simply an issue of physical representation. But Peters argued that the Mercator map symbolised power inequalities and endorsed a Eurocentric view of the world, with the more technologically advanced countries of the northern hemisphere dominating the picture. In contrast, he claimed that his physically

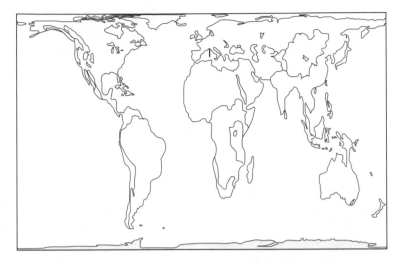

Figure 5.2 **The Peters Projection map**

more accurate version gave the less developed countries more symbolic prominence and status.

While we might call the different maps different texts, the system of values and power relationships symbolised by the texts would be called a 'discourse' by social scientists and by many literary and media scholars. In this case, the discourse would consist of not just these maps but other texts, where global politics are in evidence and where the more developed and less developed countries of the world are treated in very different ways. Even the terms 'more developed' and 'less developed' can be seen as problematic, as this way of categorising the world carries strong connotations of relative success in a rather undefined concept of progress: are people in Botswana or Malawi 'less developed' than in the UK or the USA, and, if so, how?

This meaning of 'discourse' as referring to large-scale and repeated ways of talking and writing about particular themes and topics can be traced back to the philosopher and social theorist, Michel Foucault (for a useful overview, see Rabinow 1991). Foucault's work has influenced many different academic fields due to his exploration of the idea that what we think of as 'the way things are' is a socially constructed set of discourses. Gee (1999) calls this view of discourse 'discourse with a capital D' in order to distinguish it from the smaller-scale discourse practice of analysing individual conversations. Gee's definition of 'capital D discourse' is 'language plus other stuff' (ibid.: 17). In the extensive quote below, he explains how this idea of Discourse is intimately bound up with both our individual and cultural identities:

> The key to Discourses is 'recognition'. If you put language, action, interaction, values, beliefs, symbols, objects, tools and places together in such a way that others *recognize* you as a particular type of who (identity) engaged in a particular type of what (activity) here and now, then you have pulled off a Discourse (and thereby continued it through history, if only for a while longer). Whatever you have done must be similar enough to other performances to be recognizable. However, if it is different enough from what has gone before, but still recognizable, it can simultaneously change and transform Discourses.
>
> Discourses are always embedded in a medley of social institutions, and often involve various 'props' like books and magazines of various sorts, laboratories, classrooms, buildings of various sorts, various technologies, and a myriad of other objects from sewing needles (for sewing circles) through birds (for bird watchers) to basketball courts and basketballs (for basketball players) ...
>
> It is sometimes helpful to think about social and political issues as if it is not just us humans who are talking and interacting with each other, but rather, the Discourses we represent and enact, and for which we are 'carriers'. The Discourses we enact existed before each of us came on the scene and most of them will exist long after we have left the scene. Discourses, through our words and deeds, carry on conversations with each other through history, and, in doing so, form human history.
>
> (ibid.:18)

To summarise:

- Within the English subject area (both Language and Literature), a text is likely to refer to writing, but this is not necessarily the case in other academic domains.
- While discourse analysis can refer to the small-scale analysis of spoken interaction, it can also have a much larger meaning – of ways of constructing stories about the world and communicating those stories in speech, in writing, and via behaviour that goes beyond purely linguistic expression.

- The 'big picture' idea of Discourse sees meaning as not necessarily about what individuals intend but rather about the ideas they routinely express via their cultural identities.

Narrative

When previously discussing James Joyce's novel, *Ulysses*, the phrase 'narrative devices' was used as a way of describing the variety of different strategies Joyce used in that book to tell the story. This section explores the idea of narrative in more detail.

Although we might immediately associate the idea of storytelling with literary authors, there are of course many stories we tell each other every day as a part of our interactions with others. Jokes, bits of gossip, and descriptions of events are all stories of one kind of another: as soon as there's a scene set and some action or people referred to, you have the makings of a story. Labov, mentioned in Chapter 4 with reference to accent variation, described as 'natural narratives' the stories that people told in his interviews when asked to recall a moment of danger in their lives. Labov recognised a repeated shape to their accounts: an introduction and scene setting stage, some kind of complicating action, a resolution, and a coda or conclusion that would often sum up the 'moral' or message.

Although literary texts are not the only place to find stories, researchers working in literary and media fields have explored in some detail how stories are constructed, particularly with reference to whose point of view is being expressed. In addition, literary scholars have, for obvious reasons, paid special attention to written texts; and the frameworks they have evolved to analyse literary writing can be extended to any other form of writing where participants are engaged in acts of interpretation.

A starting point for thinking about narrative is the idea of **point of view**. In everyday language, this often means 'what a person thinks'. In academic analysis, it refers more formally to whose perspective a story is told from. The place where you will have encountered this on a regular basis is in your own reading of fictive narratives, such as novels. In novels, stories are told from the perspective of one or more of the characters, or else from the perspective of someone who appears to know everything and see everything, including what's going on inside the characters' heads. The voice or persona that appears to be telling you the story is called the **narrator**, in studies of literary point of view (see Fowler 1996). Note that this figure is different from the author of a text: an author could choose to tell a story as a very different persona, for example, a male writer could create a female narrator, an adult writer could create a child narrator, and so on.

The terms 'point of view' and 'perspective', above, are based on the metaphorical idea of sight lines in a physical context. The psychological idea of whose mind you are being asked to align with is expressed via the language of physical orientation. This is familiar language in studies of literary narrative, but it is useful to observe that the literary framework is itself based on another field – that of the language of art criticism. The interconnection between physical point of view and psychological processes is obvious if you think back to the Mercator and Peters maps above. In the discussion of the maps, physical prominence translated into ideas about who was the most important – who was at the centre of things, and who was on the periphery.

Some time has been spent exploring the connection between seeing stories and telling them because these elements are not separate in our multi-sensory world: when we read (or hear) a story, we visualise actions, people, and scenes; and when we see pictures, the way the picture is organised positions us in the story it tells. For example, when you view the photograph in Figure 5.3 you are forced to look up at the Arizona butte. The position of the

Figure 5.3 **Butte in Arizona**

shot tells us something about where the photographer was standing, and as a viewer you are forced into that same viewpoint:

In studies of narrative, the narrator's choice of language (as here, the photographer's standpoint) positions or constructs the reader in that it makes assumptions about the kind of person being addressed. This constructed figure – the person who the text appears to be addressing – is called the **narratee**. As a real reader, you may or may not feel that this represents you, just as, with the photograph, you may not think that where the shot places you as a viewer offers you the best view. Readers and viewers, but especially readers, can resist the positions they are put in, as the interpretation of written language leaves so much scope for alternative readings.

Fowler (1996) summarises work on narrative point of view by grouping key aspects of narrative organisation under three broad headings: the **spatio-temporal**, **psychological**, and **ideological** points of view. These elements are not separate in how they function, but need to be focused on individually for purposes of study.

So far, discussion of point of view has referred primarily to literary fiction, but media texts such as comics, magazines, advertisements and newspaper articles, not to mention new media texts such as social networking posts, Twitter updates and online discussion forums, all involve narratives of different kinds. Newspaper stories are explicitly called 'stories' and have named authors. So everything that is said here about literary material can be applied to many media texts. In fact, since every text must of necessity have a point of view, you should be able to apply the ideas discussed here to any text, however it is classified. In English Language studies, there is no such thing as a neutral text – even material called 'information' tells a story and has a point of view.

Spatio-temporal point of view refers to the way in which stories are located in space and time. Although it might seem as if these dimensions are simply facts, spatio-temporal aspects are strongly connected with how any story works: when we tell each other stories, we often make sure to set them in a place and time; the openings of novels and also films often establish where and when the story is set – sometimes very explicitly, with place and date references such as 'London, 1980'. Then, as the story unfolds, readers and viewers have to keep track of time and place shifts as the narrative does its work. We have the specific terms 'flashback' and 'flashforward' to describe shifts in time. There are also many **adverbials** and **prepositions** that construct a sense of orientation, such as the deictic expressions 'here', 'there', 'in', 'out', 'up', 'down', and so on. They have already been discussed with reference to the chatroom data on p. 43.

The psychological point of view, in Fowler's (1996) account, refers to whose perspective the story is being told from. A story where a narrator refers to him/herself as 'I' – termed **first person narrative** because it uses the **first person pronoun** – will create a very different sense of relationship from a narrative told in the **third person**, where people and events are described from an external viewpoint, for example, via the **third person pronouns** 'he', 'she', 'it', and 'they'.

It is not possible in a book of this size to explore any particular area in detail, so you need to realise that written texts can demonstrate a great deal of subtlety in how they use apparently simple words like pronouns. For example, the use of 'we' by a large corporation, although technically first person narrative, can produce a very different kind of discourse from the 'I' of a single individual. The points of reference can also shift, as in the text below from a sandwich shop napkin. 'We' doesn't simply refer to the Pret company but their environmental department, who are presented as aligning with customers against the idea of wastefulness. (Also note the contrast being made between the terms 'serviette' and 'napkin'):

> This napkin is made from 100% recycled stock (Pret's environmental department is militant, we're making headway). If Pret staff get all serviette-ish and hand you huge bunches of napkins (which you don't need or want) please give them the evil eye. Waste not want not.

Psychological point of view might seem very different from spatio-temporal aspects, but the two are connected because the person apparently addressing you or telling the story needs to be located somewhere and communicating at a point in time. The texts in Figures 5.4, 5.5 and 5.6 illustrate this interconnectedness. They are from *99 Ways to Tell a Story* where the graphic artist, Matt Madden, opts for a different perspective and genre, or type of text, for each of the 99 times he tells the same story. The first text, called 'Template' is, as it suggests, the bare bones of the story, a set of simple events based in the characters' home. The texts that occur after the template tell the story from the point of view of, first, the fridge, then someone spying on the couple from outside.

The final aspect of narrative point of view covered by Fowler is what he calls ideology, or ideological point of view. As with the other dimensions, ideology is not a separate element, but an integral part of all the choices made

Figure 5.4 **Template**
Source: Madden (2005).

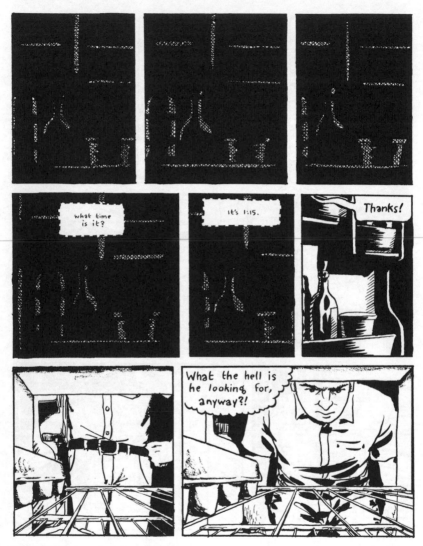

Figure 5.5 A refrigerator with a view
Source: Madden (2005).

Figure 5.6 **Voyeur**
Source: Madden (2005).

about how the narrative should be told. Ideology refers to belief systems, attitudes and values; and choices about who should tell the story, as well as when and where they are communicating, are a both a reflection and construction of a world view. Those textual choices assume that you, as a reader, hold certain beliefs, attitudes and values – in short, that you are a particular kind of narratee.

Studies of narrative can involve the analysis of many different aspects of language. For example, whether an account is written in the **active** or **passive voice** can profoundly alter how the participants and events are viewed. The work of Hoey (2000), Simpson (1993) and Toolan (2001) focus specifically on written texts, and deal with many different aspects of language. The related field of critical discourse analysis, which aims explicitly to uncover how power is brokered in texts and discourses of all kinds, is exemplified by the work of Fairclough (2001).

Semiotics and representation

De Saussure's original idea about language was that elements exist in a system of inter-relationships. In this system, he claimed that each feature was defined as much by what it wasn't as by what it was: so, for example, a /b/ sound is a /b/ partly because it is not a /p/ sound. Although in English the sounds are produced in the same manner and place in the mouth, /b/ has **voice** while /p/ does not.

De Saussure saw the language system as working in the same way as other systems that we see as meaningful, saying that we needed to develop a 'science of signs', or semiology, in order to understand them. He saw language as a system or code where choices of individual **signs** from the code are significant, and where principles of combination are as important as selection.

This way of thinking about human communication systems and meaning came to be called **structuralism** because of its interpretation of the world in structural terms. This is now seen as one way of thinking among others, attracting some criticism over the years for what can appear to be a rather fixed notion of meaning, but the area of semiotics has been influential both within English Language – for example, in Halliday's idea of language as a 'social semiotic' – and in other academic subjects, particularly in the Media Studies and **Cultural Studies** fields.

Some awareness of semiotics is important for students of English Language because of the inter-relationship between verbal language and other communicative systems. At the most basic level, semiotics analyses the way signs work, distinguishing different relationships between the sign itself and what it refers to. De Saussure saw linguistic signs as **arbitrary** – that there is no intrinsic connection between a word and its **referent**, or the thing it represents, beyond the connection established by cultural convention. In the same way, semioticians would see no connection beyond convention for representing love with a heart, or romance with a rose. However, they would claim that signs such as these carry considerable connotative power and are embedded in cultural contexts, so an analysis of how they work is necessary to an understanding of language and culture (one of the English Language benchmarks).

As with the areas of discourse and narrative, there is considerable detail to explore in semiotics, including how closely any one sign mirrors its referent. For example, the term 'icon' is often used to refer to a sign that is a copy of its referent (such as a photograph), while 'index' reflects, as it suggests, an indication (smoke is an index of fire) and 'symbol' an arbitrary representation (such as an owl, for wisdom). (See Chandler 2002, for a useful overview.)

As well as the analysis of smaller items such as logos, Media Studies scholarship has sometimes applied semiotic concepts to much larger texts, such as films and TV programmes. For example, the TV programme, *Big Brother*, where contestants are constantly under surveillance while they live in a specially constructed world, takes its title from George Orwell's *1984*, where 'big brother' was an autocratic ruler. Seeing links between cultural artefacts such as TV programmes while understanding how the connections are being reconfigured is a semiotic activity because it explores popular meaning-making. The focus on everyday activities is also at the core of Cultural Studies, where the exploration might also consider more explicitly issues of power, social class and hegemony (cultural and political domination). For example, are we being fed surveillance as entertainment in order to accept more surveillance in our real lives?

These questions may seem a long way away from language issues, but language is often centre stage where connections are being made between texts. The phenomenon of intertextuality, associated with the critical theorists, Mikhail Bakhtin (1981), and Julia Kristeva (Moi 1986), refers to the way one text can refer to another, bringing echoes from the history of use of a particular word or phrase. For example, the text in Figure 5.7 is from a UK car park, reminding those who have parked their cars to pay at the ticket machine.

On the exit gate of the car park was Figure 5.8. This second text refers intertextually to the first one, reversing the 'pay and display' word order and completely changing the meaning, from paying for a ticket to losing one's

Figure 5.7 'Pay and display' car park sign

valuables to passing thieves. The similarity to the first text makes the police warning possibly a confusing read on first viewing, while readers work out the puzzle, but perhaps that is the point – a puzzle has to be solved, and requires attention. The danger might be that readers just think it is the same text as the first one, and pass by without heeding it.

Intertextual references can be a lot more subtle than this example, but whatever the strength of the intertextuality, they assume cultural knowledge on the part of the reader, with items such as song lyrics, advertising hooks, the titles of TV programmes, novels, and idiomatic phrases often being recycled for their ability to set up echoes of their former use. But intertextual relationships raise interesting questions about the potential responses of different audiences to the same text, particularly the value to writers of phrases which some people might not understand. They also raise rather more

Figure 5.8 'Display and pay' police notice

philosophical questions about the nature of originality and creativity in language. While Chomsky saw creativity in language as the ability to use a finite set of items to produce an infinite set of utterances, Bakhtin's model of language is as a shared cultural resource where language is re-purposed to suit new contexts and to create different speaking positions or viewpoints in texts. Creativity is then more about artful recycling than about brand new expressions.

The concept of representation occurs frequently in literary and media analyses and is closely connected with semiotics because it is all about how things appear. Earlier the term 'representation' was used in the discussion of the relationship between words and the mental images they might produce in our minds. Representation as used in this chapter is more socially oriented, referring to the ways in which aspects of our lives – people, things, activities, ideas – are presented in the texts that surround us. The term representation was used in this way, too, on

p. 21, where the connotations of 'Frenchness' were discussed with reference to perfume names. The two meanings of representation – mental images and social expression – are of course mutually shaping.

Representation is an important concept in the discussion of how different social groups are described and viewed. The language used to label and define groups is often under scrutiny as part of considering the role language plays in discrimination. 'Political correctness' (if you are against the idea of changing language) and 'language reform' (if you are in favour of it) are topics which are explored in academic books and papers – for example, Cameron (1995) looks at how this theme is treated in public discourses such as newspapers.

Representation is about more than just gender, but language and gender is one area where there is now a long tradition of **feminist** critique (see Cameron 1998, for an overview). Researchers have looked particularly at the kinds of texts that might be considered trivial by some people – such as popular romance stories, forms of advertising, and personal ads – and observed repeated patterns of representation in the depiction of male and female figures (see Harvey and Shalom 1997; Goddard and Mean 2009). The focus on the kinds of texts that surround us every day is important, as these are not only giving us frequent messages about ourselves and others, but also we take them in without too much conscious thought as we go about our busy lives. As an illustration of gender and representation, but also of other aspects of representation, look at the two advertisements in Figures 5.9 and 5.10, from an airport hoarding in Bangkok. In thinking about how you would analyse texts such as these, you might also recall the earlier coverage of narrative and consider what stories are being told here, and how. The texts are advertising a company called *The Wall Street Institute School of English*, which sells English language tuition in 26 countries and is owned by Pearson, a multinational corporation with many educational businesses, including the UK exam board, Edexcel.

Stylistics

So far, the focus of this chapter has been on concepts and approaches that are commonly used in literary and media fields, thinking about how these ideas could be applied to studies in English Language. But the relationship can also work the other way: if a student of English Language is interested in the way literature, in particular, works, then the area of Stylistics offers many ideas. Stylistics is primarily concerned with studying the language of literary texts,

Figure 5.9 Wall Street cool, billboard advertising Wall Street English in Thailand

Figure 5.10 Wall Street hot

although more recently it has begun to address texts beyond that category (see Simpson 2004, for more detail).

The aspects already mentioned, such as narrative, ideology, semiotics and representation, are all relevant to literary texts, of course. Stylistics is less interested in literature in the sense of specific literary authors – although some researchers have specialised in looking at particular writers or genres – and more interested in how literary texts work as pieces of communication. This might involve, for example, looking at how literary texts represent dialogue between characters. People studying English Language are likely to have a good understanding of real speech, and will be able to see how literary authors have constructed representations of the real thing. Such students are then unlikely to fall into the trap of calling literary dialogue 'realistic'. This not only applies to how interactions are represented, but also to the way in which literary writers might vary the **orthographic** (spelling) system in order to suggest the accent of the narrator or the characters. Unpicking how this is constructed involves looking at the **grapho-phonemic** relationships between sounds and alphabetic symbols. Linguists use phonetic symbols in order to transcribe sounds as accurately as possible, but literary writers often change the alphabetic letters around in words to simulate pronunciation.

The techniques mentioned above are not simply the province of literary texts, but can be found in media texts where the intention is to simulate and/or personalise the spoken voice in a playful way. For example, Figure 5.11 shows a Google ad which manipulates the conventional alphabet to get readers to say 'arrival times' to themselves. The ad is for Google's voice facility for mobile phones, whereby a phone owner can speak a request into the phone rather than typing it in: this particular ad was placed on a railway station, so the focus here is on the idea of getting train arrival times.

Written phonetically, as a linguist would transcribe it, this line would have looked like this (if spoken using a Received Pronunciation English accent):

əraɪvəl taɪmz

but then the mass audience would not have understood it.

Literary fiction can sometimes be written at some length using representations of dialect, such as Irvine Welsh's *Trainspotting* or Alice Walker's *Color Purple*. Fiction can also suggest the idea of new meanings

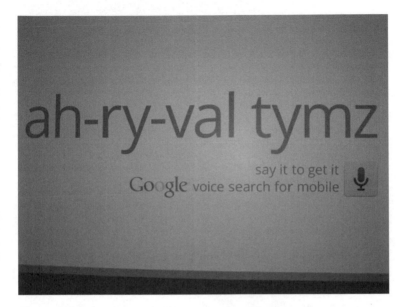

Figure 5.11 A Google advertisement. Top of image

for existing language, or wholly new languages, such as the 'Newspeak' of Orwell's *1984*, Anthony Burgess's Russian-based 'Nadsat' in *A Clockwork Orange*, or Suzette Haden Elgin's 'Láaden', the female-oriented language of her *Mother Tongue* novels. In these cases, it is interesting to work out how the writers manage to convince readers that the meanings or language they are using are new, without completely baffling them. A similar question could be asked about how the language works in 'nonsense' poetry. In fact, can language ever be completely meaningless?

The list of possible explorations of literary and media representations of 'reality' is potentially very long. Anywhere that a constructed text is purporting to be 'real life', there are opportunities for language enthusiasts to analyse how texts have been artfully shaped, from their knowledge of the texts and discourses that exist in the 'non-literary' category.

Ultimately, there is an opportunity to think about these categories themselves: is there such a thing as 'literariness' in language, or do we call something literary because it is marketed to us in that way? Or have we wrongly described ordinary language as rather dull and uninteresting, when in fact it is full of the same kinds of creative play as we see on the stage?

In whose interests is it to have these categories in the first place? And is everything changing anyway because we can all 'publish' ourselves on the Web? There are no easy answers to these questions but researching them can take us on an interesting journey.

6

Areas of Creative Writing

Creative Writing as an academic subject has developed rapidly in recent years. However, as was the case with the previous chapter, this chapter is not about what you might do if you go to study the subject in its own right. Rather, the aim of this chapter is to consider how some of the approaches and activities that are characteristic of Creative Writing courses can contribute to an understanding of language. As was the case with the study of literary and media texts, the benchmark statements recognise that some English Language courses may draw on aspects of Creative Writing in order to develop students' awareness and skills in particular areas.

Benchmark statements

The following statements for English Language refer particularly to ideas and activities that are common on Creative Writing courses:

The nature and scope of the subject

- awareness of the implications of language choices and of the cultural, literary and historical context in which the texts were produced.

Course coverage

- the way language choices construct different genres, registers, and styles.

Subject-related skills

- critical skills in the close reading, description, analysis, or production of texts or discourses;
- responsiveness to the central role of language in the creation of meaning and a sensitivity to the affective power of language.

Creativity and criticality

Creative writing in an academic context is not necessarily just about writing well. It can also be about using creative writing activities as a tool for critical awareness – hence the sub-heading above. The idea is that because language is so familiar to us and the repeated discourses that surround us seem so natural, a creative approach can help us to see things afresh.

A practical example of the kind of approach that is possible is called 'textual intervention' by Pope (1995). This covers many different activities, but all with the aim of using creative writing tasks in order to generate a new and alternative view of the text you are investigating. An existing text might be rewritten from a different narrative viewpoint, such as having a different character telling the story. Or it might be set in a different time or place, or produced in a different genre, using a different mode, or with a different purpose or audience in mind. Each shift changes the perspective of the text and therefore its ideological stance. The ultimate aim is to develop students' critical awareness of the power and significance of language choices in texts of all kinds.

The idea of shifting perspectives has in fact been a long-standing tradition in the work of published authors. For example, Jean Rhys takes a figure called Bertha from Charlotte Brontë's *Jane Eyre*, to tell the story in her novel, *The Wide Sargasso Sea* (1966). In both books, the Bertha figure is Mr Rochester's first wife, but is renamed 'Antoinette' in Rhys's novel, and narrates her own history in the Caribbean and then the UK as a mixed race woman. In *Jane Eyre*, this figure features as an unexplained 'madwoman in the attic' who eventually sets fire to the house. Rhys elaborates her background and early life, seeing her as a victimised figure who suffers inequality at the hands of a white patriarchal society. Changing the perspective of the narrative, then, allows a completely different story to be told and one that explicitly addresses issues of race and colonial politics.

Jean Rhys's reworked narrative is a good example of what the benchmark statements (above) mean when they refer to awareness of the 'cultural, literary and historical contexts' of texts. But this awareness can be developed without a detailed knowledge of literature. All cultures have well-known stories – fairy tales, folk tales, urban myths, stories by nationally known and cele- brated writers – that have become culturally shared knowledge. These stories, too, rehearse ideas that can be revealed and then challenged via creative activities. For example, Angela Carter's writing shows how the reworking of fairly tales can radically challenge representations of gender: her Little Red Riding Hood, in *The Company of Wolves* (1981), finds the 'wolf' a much more attractive prospect than the dull boys of her village. A similar 'make- over' is currently being given to the vampire figure in popular stories in the UK and the USA.

Linking the activity of creative writing with ideas about representation enables students of English Language, as well as students of all the other academic fields mentioned in Chapters 4–7, to see how language is a powerful tool for meaning-making. As a small example of what can be revealed, look at the extract below, originally taken from a *Mills and Boon* romance, and reproduced in a longer form in Goddard and Mean (2009). In this passage, all the pronouns have been reversed, producing a very different representation from the original depiction of seduction. In this reworked version, the woman is predatory and the man is the anxious prey:

'You know what I'm talking about'. She was oddly elated, her eyes flashing down at him, her mouth curling at the edges with satisfaction.

Nervously he shook his head, the swing of his blond hair against his cheek catching her eye. She shifted her hand to it, thrusting her fingers among the strands, winnowing them slowly and watching the way they drifted against her flesh.

'Don't lie to me, even if you've been lying to yourself'. Urgency deepened her voice and he felt a surge of panic begin inside him. 'Ever since I saw you at that window…'

'No', he broke out, turning stumblingly away.

(*Seduction,* Charlotte Lamb, p. 64)

In this section, the idea of creativity has been seen as very wide-ranging and something we all have the potential to develop, rather than some quality of rare genius. As exemplified here, being creative can be as much about re-fashioning material to create new perspectives – in other words, using intertextuality – as about a notion of complete originality. The question of what exactly creativity is, is rather too large to be explored in any detail here. But it is important to note that for some scholars – for example, Bakhtin, mentioned earlier – there is no such thing as language that has no history or context of use, in which case, creativity is all about skilful re-arrangement.

Creative writing activities described so far are about using creativity to enhance critical awareness, but there are also many creative tasks that you might see more as developing your personal communication skills. The general expectation in academic circles would be that the better your critical skills, the more thoughtful and precise a language user you will be.

Chapters 10 and 11 will focus on how to showcase the communication skills you have acquired and relate them to professional careers, where there will be very job-specific writing demands. Whatever the particular writing tasks you have as part of your professional context – whether that's writing advertising copy or school reports, news articles or academic papers – a fundamental requirement is a critical awareness of genres, or text types, and an ability to adapt them in creative ways.

Genre

The term 'genre' means slightly different things in different subject areas. In Literary Studies, it has tended to mean different types of literary text – poetry, drama, prose fiction – as well as particular subdivisions, such as detective fiction, science fiction, romance, and so on. In Media Studies, 'genre' has also been used to distinguish between different conventions, for example, Western, Thriller, and Horror films.

In English Language study, genre will have a much wider definition, encompassing all kinds of texts and discourses, and including speech as well as writing. A wider focus will go beyond literary or media texts and think about everyday local examples like a shopping list or a birthday party, as well as more officially recognised texts and events such as legal documents and wedding ceremonies. The approach to genre taken by different Creative Writing courses may vary in terms of its scope and degree of 'literariness'. But, increasingly, tutors planning and delivering writing courses and activities are thinking more carefully about how the skills associated with writing in literary contexts can be generalised across all types of communication.

The English Language benchmarks talk of 'the way language choices construct different genres, registers and styles', and this may seem at first glance to be a simple matter to observe and produce. But the fact is that good writing will be alive to change, so making choices is by no means just about following a set formula. This might just work in a will or a wedding ceremony, where legal definitions are fixed and the demands of ritual are high, although even here, definitions can change and rituals be adapted.

The terms 'genre', 'register', and 'style' are themselves subject to different definitions and, certainly, genre can be particularly difficult to pin down. The explanations above are just a starting point. The term 'genre' can encompass all of the following (based on Beard 2001):

- *The formal aspects of the text or discourse*, such as the use of specific layouts, or lexis. The term 'register' refers to field-specific terms, and a genre may have strong connections with a particular semantic field. An example would be a medical report.
- *The function of the text or discourse.* All texts will have a function, and a genre grouping could be based on their main purpose, for example, to persuade, as in the case of advertisements, political speeches, and public notices.
- *The response sought.* The examples above expect a certain kind of response on the part of the receivers, to change their behaviour or thinking.
- *How a text or discourse is understood by readers and listeners/viewers*: if you tell a joke or do an impression of someone, and your audience doesn't recognise what you are doing, have you remained in the genres of 'joke' and 'impression', respectively?
- *The audience being targeted.* Some texts are very audience specific, for example, books for children, or notices for hotel guests. These texts are likely to involve a particular style – in the case of hotel guests, this is often very formal. A hotel notice would be unlikely to say 'Get a move on when you leave, otherwise you'll really mess things up for us ...'
- *The setting of the communication.* A school classroom discussion might involve a 'hands-up' routine, but you wouldn't do this when having a discussion with friends in a café or pub.
- *The relationship between the participants.* Some genres are predicated, for example, on a power difference between interlocutors. This would be the case in an interview, or courtroom examination.

The questions above are important because they have real-life applications and implications. The ways in which we understand the concept of genre in the descriptions above are culture specific, involving understanding of how things are categorised and 'how things are done' in a particular culture. Thinking about genres involves thinking about the forms of cultural knowledge that underlie acts of communication. This is an essential part of anyone's communication skills.

To explore genre in a more anthropological way, think about how food shops organise their products in your culture. You might think about supermarkets, where a wide range of food is on offer, or about different kinds of specialist shops that you have in your area. How much cultural knowledge do you need in order to manage your shopping, in these contexts? For example, if you focus on a supermarket, what different genres of foodstuff do they have? What goes with what? What headings are used, for the aisles? Are some things classified in unexpected and confusing ways? If you are focusing on different shops, what knowledge do you need in order to understand which type of shop sells which products?

When you answered the questions above, you were actively describing genres as they operate in your culture. You probably found yourself questioning why things were organised in that way, and realising that you have a lot of cultural knowledge that you carry around in your head. But what happens when you encounter something where you are an outsider? In order to think that through, try listing all the things you need to know about in order to understand the sign in Figure 6.1, which was on the bank of a river in Canada.

The complex cultural knowledge and rules that we have to be aware of in order to understand and produce genres is not fixed, because societies change all the time. We want to adapt old genres and create new ones as part of meeting the demands of new communication contexts. Also, part of human creativity

Figure 6.1 **Canadian riverside sign**

involves rule-breaking and refreshing our ideas of how to communicate. An important aspect of any inputs from creative writers – defined not just as 'literary authors' but as 'writers who take a creative approach' – is to help you develop your own thinking about communication, both as a topic and as a skill.

Figure 6.2 is Matt Madden's rule-breaking skill in action, adapting his 'Template' from *Exercises in Style* (see Figure 5.4) to the genre of an emergency notice.

Figure 6.2 Exercises in style
Source: Madden (2005).

Multimodality and new technologies

It would be remiss in a book on English Language and its associated fields not to address the recent changes in communication that have developed as a result of new technologies. These changes have already made some of the terms we use to describe communication a bit problematic. One example of this is that new digital genres cannot be simply described as either writing, or speech-like, because they often have qualities of both (Goddard 2004). In types of computer-mediated communication such as blogs, discussion forums, instant messaging, social networking sites, and websites of all kinds, written text can be accompanied by images, video and sound. This makes a label like 'creative writing' not very accurate if what is being studied and developed is **multimodal** communication.

Multimodality means using more than one mode at a time and some would argue that this was an aspect of communication long before the advent of computers, since even a picture with a caption required decoding different types of text and understanding one message in terms of another. However, it is generally recognised that digital texts require new sorts of skills both to read and to construct, because they no longer conform to the kind of linearity readers expect from a paper-based text. Reading text on a computer (or now on mobile phones, as many of these have web applications) allows a non-linear approach, where readers use links to move from one page to another, determining their own pathways to get to the information they need. Termed 'new literacy' as a result of the new practices involved (Street and Lefstein 2007), the skills to operate in new digital environments include the ability to sort and critique many different sources of information and produce text at high speed for rapid consumption by unknown others.

New environments radically challenge older certainties about audience, since we are in effect publishing ourselves to the digitised world; about memory and history, since our new technological capacities allow us to archive massive amounts of data; and about privacy and surveillance, since we leave digital trails of our existence everywhere we go. Above all, the global nature of new environments means that we are potentially in contact with more people from different cultures, which is all to the good. But communicating with others who are doubly unknown to us (at a physical remove, and also from a different culture) requires more skill in intercultural communication, and an understanding of the fluid nature of identities. Where the communication medium is English, online contexts present a new site for the development of English as a lingua franca.

Figure 6.3 Lolcat image

New communication environments present many opportunities for language research, as well as sites for the creation of texts. Figure 6.3 gives an example of how the two elements of creativity and critical analysis often co-exist in language users' own practices as well as in academic domains. The image is from an internet site called 'I can has cheezburger' http://icanhascheezburger.com where communities of users post up photos of their cats and add their own captions, using a made-up language called 'LOLspeak'. The captions have to obey the rules of LOLspeak, which are complex, and are voted on, for their ability to offer a humorous and relevant perspective. The photos are tagged, creating a **folksonomy** in the same way as YouTube or Flickr.

The website may seem like a frivolous pursuit that doesn't have much to do with serious study or skill. But it can also be seen, and researched, as a contemporary example in a long tradition of playing with language, showing the power of language to connect complete strangers via shared humour. The complex language of LOLspeak takes skill to learn and use creatively, reflected in the aesthetic judgements made by others as they vote for the best examples. Researching why some examples are seen as better than others would reveal not just attitudes to humour but also participants' awareness of the grammar of this new language.

The LOLcats phenomenon made the UK national press in the general election of 2010, when pictures of Nick Clegg, the now deputy Prime Minister, were given LOLspeak captions by witty commentators (see Goddard and Geesin 2011). But LOLcats is no flash in the pan. It has generated a huge range of products, from t-shirts to dictionaries of LOLspeak. The network of humour sites of which it is a part (there are versions of LOLcats using photos of other kinds of animals) has 375 million page views and 110 million video views per month, with its current 16.5 million visitors uploading 500,000 pictures and videos. In January 2011, the company attracted investors to the tune of $30 million (Gannes 2011). This shows how an understanding of language, communication, and creativity can be a serious business.

7

Metalanguage

Benchmark statements

The following statements for English Language refer to particular aspects of study where metalanguage will be given emphasis:

Course coverage

- structural aspects of contemporary English;
- how English might be compared with other languages.

Analytical techniques

- study samples of text in terms of analytical frameworks ranging from segmental phonetics to the structure and nature of discourses;
- analyse underlying language systems at all levels of language, from phonetic to semantic.

Metalanguage means 'language about language'. In everyday discourse, we do not just use language, we also reflect on it as we go along. For example, we might say in the middle of telling someone a story 'to cut a long story short' or write in an essay, 'to summarise' (see p. 54 in this book). These phrases, which can be described as **discourse markers**, express an evaluation by a speaker or writer of their own language use – that what they are saying has got a bit long-winded or complicated, and needs some kind of remedial action.

This is one kind of metalanguage, but there are others. You have seen already by the number of glossed items in this book that the academic areas being covered have their own concepts and categories that have a vocabulary attached to them. In fact, each academic area will have its own discourse, made distinctive by a focus on particular themes and the adoption of particular perspectives. Just as medical researchers have a language to talk about medicine, so language researchers have a language to talk about language.

The precise metalanguage that accompanies any study of English Language will depend on the nature of the programme; and it is also likely that different modules within a programme will have their own specialist vocabulary, simply because English Language is a very broad subject and can be made up of different elements. For example, there may be modules or units with a very scientific orientation and others with an arts orientation, in which case you need to be prepared for a different experience in each case. However, there should also be a great deal of common vocabulary that is shared and that recurs across programmes.

So far, this book has attempted to give what would be termed a 'big picture' of English Language study, focusing on large-scale areas like Sociolinguistics, Literary Studies, and so on. But there are also ways of looking at language which are more micro-focused and concerned with the linguistic ingredients of communication. The value of having a vocabulary to talk about language in this case is to enable a researcher to point precisely to a linguistic item and cite it as evidence of how a text or discourse works, or why one theory seems convincing and another does not. A micro-focus can also sometimes help to explain larger questions about human behaviour and attitudes.

One area of focus commonly covered on English Language courses is that of Phonetics and Phonology. This was referred to briefly in Chapter 4. While phonetics refers to the study of the physical aspects of sound production and reception, such as how sound is produced (**articulatory** phonetics), phonology is a more abstract study of the sound system of a language. The former area potentially has many applications in health and medicine, not least in therapeutic work with individuals who through accident, illness or birth defect, have difficulty producing sounds and have to learn new strategies or re-learn old ones. Although the basis of the area of phonetics is sound, not all individuals communicate acoustically – British sign language users interact visually. This can also be studied at a micro-level, exploring the different signs that act as the base units of the language.

Although the main focus of study in English Language is English, that does not mean that aspects of how other languages work will not come into play.

Comparing English with other languages can enable some understanding of a range of different issues, such as why people might have difficulty pronouncing certain sounds in English or in other languages. It can also throw some light on attitudes to language, helping you to take a more dispassionate look at how language is often used in representations of group identity, and in arguments about social behaviour. For example, Chinese speakers of English sometimes confuse /l/ and /r/ sounds, because these sounds are not seen as distinctively different in Mandarin – they are seen as variants (**allophones**) of the same **phoneme**, or sound unit. This difficulty is often the focus of stereotypical representations of Chinese speakers of English. Although it does not explain why people stereotype others, knowing about sounds in this case can reveal something of the mechanism by which the stereotype is constructed. This in turn can help to explain why the stereotype persists – it fixes on a real aspect of speech, tapping into what can actually be heard by the speakers being asked to recognise the stereotype.

If a similar stereotype were to operate in the opposite direction, with Mandarin speakers fixing on a sound that English speakers get wrong, it could well be the sound /p/, which in Mandarin is seen as two phonemes, one where it is **aspirated**, as in the word 'pin', and one where it is not, as in the word 'spin' (Trask 1999: 232). While English speakers would hardly hear the difference between these sounds, a Mandarin speaker will hear them as quite separate sounds and they can sometimes produce two completely different word meanings.

Studying the phonological level of English can also tell us much about English regional speech, and therefore about differences between real speech and how it is represented in texts such as novels, comics, cartoons, and so on. Different regional speakers may have different phoneme inventories, or numbers of sounds, in their variety of English. If speakers are aware of prestige varieties of accent and try to adapt accordingly, this can be seen in phonetic transcriptions of their speech. The phenomenon of **hypercorrection**, where a speaker overcompensates for their own perceptions of difference between their own variety and a prestige norm, can be revealed in this way.

Discussion so far has been of units of sound, or phonemes, but connected speech is more than a sum of individual sounds. Speech has what is termed **prosody**, or aspects that flow across speech, such as intonation and rhythm. These features are sometimes called **suprasegmental** because they exist above the level of segments, or individual sounds. Being able to produce the right prosodic contour for an utterance is an important aspect of being understood. We have probably all failed to understand an utterance at some point because, although the speaker had all the right words occurring in the right order, the **stress** they put on words or the **intonation** they used was wrong. Researchers in the field of artificial intelligence (AI) are constantly addressing this issue, and you might have perceived some of the difficulties they face when you have heard or interacted with machines designed to produce and/or comprehend speech, such as railway companies' digitised messages on trains, the voice of your satnav (GPS), the speech recognition software used by call centres, or the voice-to-text tools used on computers and mobile devices. Aside from the obvious therapeutic applications for the AI field, there are clearly many aspects of everyday life where we can accomplish predictable routines with the help of machines that can recognise human speech and/or produce a simulated version of it.

In studying sounds, you may be introduced to the **International Phonetic Alphabet** (IPA), which is a way of writing down the sounds that speakers produce, and it has a variety of applications. It differs from the normal written alphabet in that it is not based on the spelling system, but reflects how sounds are actually produced. In English, there are 26 letters in the alphabet we use for writing, but about 44 different sounds that occur in speech (depending on your accent), so there is no straightforward one-to-one correspondence between sound and symbol. To illustrate this idea, look at the words below, which all have 'ough' in their spelling, but which all have different pronunciations:

> through
> cough
> tough
> ought
> plough

You saw some transcription in action on pp. 68–69, illustrating the difference between an advertiser's attempt to use the conventional alphabet to represent sound, and a phonemic version. That transcript would be called phonetic if it had tried to capture in a more precise way how an individual actually pronounced 'arrival times'.

The IPA has many real-world uses, for example, in training people how to speak or sing in a foreign language, in showing readers how to pronounce words they have looked up in a dictionary, in allowing speech therapists to write down what a child is saying in order to analyse their speech difficulties, and in forensic studies of accent. It may seem challenging to learn at first, but acquiring a facility with it repays the effort involved.

The **graphological** aspects of language include written symbols and other aspects of visual layout. Confusingly, graphology can refer to handwriting analysis, but this is a different meaning from the term that would be used in language study. Handwriting analysts who call themselves graphologists attempt to infer certain psychological characteristics from the way someone writes – so they may say someone has an aggressive or introverted personality, for example. This is not the kind of activity that a study of English Language would involve. There are language-trained forensic scientists who might be asked to look at samples of writing, but their work would involve matching the samples, or not, on the basis of the evidence. This activity would be called forensic document examination and could involve not just handwriting (or, more likely, typefaces and fonts these days) but other aspects of the data.

A graphological focus on written language within English Language study could range from an exploration of the early writing of young children and their mastery of alphabetic letters all the way up to the semiotics of how texts appear, including their use of colour, logos, and other meaningful aspects. Although English Language study may focus primarily on verbal language, it is difficult to separate words and phrases from other aspects of the communication, whether that is the way written text looks and its use of images, or, in speech, the non-verbal messages that are produced.

To illustrate the graphological level of language, look at the different layouts in Figure 7.1, and decide what type of text each of these might be – you don't have to name each text exactly, just suggest a possible genre. You will quickly see from this exercise that you already have considerable knowledge of the graphological conventions of different genres and can start to identify them even without knowing what they say.

Further areas of English Language study where you are likely to encounter a particular metalanguage include lexis and morphology, syntax and grammar.

The term lexis has already been used in this book, to describe aspects of vocabulary in Chapter 4. Lexicographers work on the production of dictionaries, constantly finding ways to track changes in word meaning and collect popular usage of new terms that come into the language. The 'word', however, is not the smallest unit of meaning: this is the **morpheme**. A morpheme can be as small as a single letter, for example, the 's' on 'cats' is meaningful in English because it tells us that the word has a plural referent, i.e. more than one cat is being referred to.

Another related term is **lexeme**, which describes a cluster of variants that are all related. If we take the word 'eat', for example, we don't think of 'eats'

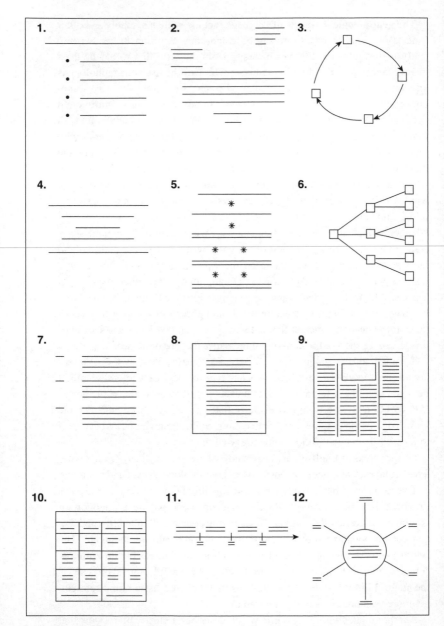

Figure 7.1 Layouts

or 'eating' as unrelated items, but as variants of each other, with the central item 'eat' as the base form, or **lemma**.

Lexis and morphology were listed alongside syntax and grammar because these aspects of language are inter-related, and you may find that you are studying them in an integrated way – or, if not, then you should know that they can be connected. The morphemes above – the 's' on 'cats' and on 'eats' – give grammatical information: the 's' on cats tells us that the **noun** is plural, and the 's' on 'eats' could suggest a plural noun, as in 'they had some eats'. The 's' on 'eats' could also be a form of the **verb** used in the third person – he, she, or it 'eats'. In each case, then, the morphology of the word is strongly connected with grammar, or the structural rules that govern how words and phrases relate to each other.

The 'morph' in morphology means 'shape', and the term morphology can be seen in other academic fields, such as in biology, where it refers to bodily structure. Morphology can be seen as one aspect of grammar because the precise shapes of words – for example, whether the word is cat, or cats, above – is connected with grammatical rules, in this case, the rules for plurality in English. But grammar also includes word order and sentence structure, which is the province of syntax. Word order is significant in English – the two examples below consist of exactly the same words but the reversal of order completely changes the meaning, with only the second example being a newsworthy headline:

Cat eats fish
Fish eats cat

These aspects of language are areas where you are already an expert, because you use the structures that are being described here. What you may not know is the metalanguage, and it is important to recognise that difference and distinction. When people say 'I don't know any grammar', or 'I was never taught grammar', they are referring to the labels for linguistic structures, not the structures themselves. We all learn the structures by communicating with others around us as we grow up, and this is such a natural process that we are not even aware that we know them.

Studying grammar as an academic subject is different from the way you learnt the grammatical structures of your first language as a child. It is about learning some of the different strategies that have been suggested for the labelling of language structures. There is no one grammar in the sense of one labelling system, but many different grammars as various groups of scholars over the years have suggested different methods. For example, Chomsky's generative grammar was discussed earlier as a way to account for his idea that language was part of our general cognitive processes. A type of grammatical analysis called **systemic-functional grammar**, developed particularly by Halliday (2004), emphasises the social function of language, suggesting that language systems and choices have ideational (content-oriented), interpersonal (relationship-oriented) and textual (text-oriented) functions. Another type of grammatical analysis, called **construction grammar**, relates more to the idea of scripts and schemas that was discussed in Chapter 5.

The point of studying grammar, then, is not to take a **prescriptive** approach to language and arbitrate over 'correct' usage, but to think about to what extent different grammatical models offer useful explanations of how language works and is used. The emphasis on usage is known as a **descriptive** approach.

Grammatical analysis can be applied in many ways, including helping us understand how language is used to express nuances of meaning and attitude. Grammatical patterning can be observed in texts of all kinds, from SMS to literary works, from political speeches to advertising, and from sports reporting to instruction manuals. This aspect of metalanguage needs to be seen as a tool for researching how language works, not as a catalogue of terms. And as with any tool, a grammatical analysis needs to be employed where it is appropriate.

To illustrate the essential idea that grammar is about language use, look at the example below. This will exemplify how you use your grammatical knowledge – your knowledge of how language structures fit together – to make sense of the messages you encounter in everyday life. This is the wording from the front of a packet of ham bought from a supermarket on 2 August 2011. As you work out what goes with what in this description, you are using your grammatical knowledge of an area called modification – the descriptive terms that give you more information about an item, in this case the word 'ham':

British Free Range Dry Cured Molasses Roast Hampshire Gammon Ham

While your knowledge of grammar will have helped you to work out the possible relationships between the modifiers above, your awareness of semantics also helped you to get a sense of the overall meaning of this string of words. In Chapter 4, the term semantics was used in association with word meaning, and the idea of connotation, or associative meaning, was seen as a strong element in how we might understand language. But the overall meaning of this line of words is more than the individual meaning of each word, added together. The overall meaning or semantic needs knowledge of ways of writing and talking – the level of language we termed 'Discourse' in Chapter 5. In this case, the discourse is not just of food but of a particular kind of food and a perspective on it, the idea of food with a pedigree, sourced from an identified rural area of Britain, from livestock that roamed free, and prepared by several labour-intensive processes. This ham was an expensive product – gammon ham is a prized cut – and the language helps to justify that expense by suggesting just how much work has gone into its production.

Of course, there was more significance in the language in its original context than this line, stripped away from the packaging and layout, can convey. In fact the first three words were in bolder type, and the whole text was in a handwritten typeface similar to this:

British Free Range Dry Cured Molasses Roast Hampshire Gammon Ham

Although the analysis of this example, then, is far from complete, it should be clear that grammatical knowledge is one type of knowledge that language users employ to understand messages, and that it works alongside other aspects. A further question might be, how much real-world knowledge – of cuts of ham, of types of ham production, of types of supermarket – is involved in understanding language at this discursive level? Should this book have photographed the packaging and presented the whole thing, including how the item was placed and displayed? Some thoughts about authenticity and sources will be addressed in Research Methods (Chapter 9).

8

Interdisciplinarity and Applied Studies

Benchmark statement

The following statement for English Language refers particularly to inter-disciplinary work:

Course coverage

- how language analyses can be applied in real world contexts, such as education, business, the law, performance arts, intercultural negotiations, politics, and the media.

Interdisciplinarity refers to the idea of establishing connections between different academic subject areas. This should already be a familiar idea from the way in which English Language is able to draw on the fields covered so far – Linguistics, Literary and Media Studies, Creative Writing.

This chapter goes further afield, exploring how ideas from English Language can be applied to some quite diverse contexts. Some of the examples in the benchmark statement above have academic discourses of their own, and the idea of interdisciplinarity is not to expect students to add another huge field of knowledge to their existing studies. Rather, the idea is to apply the concepts and tools of English Language to the fields covered by other disciplines, in order to offer some insights into the nature and role of language in those fields. The reference to 'real world contexts' in the statement above is not meant to imply that being academic is different from being in the real world.

It refers to the idea that English Language can be applied to the work contexts that those subjects relate to – such as teaching, marketing and management, the legal system, entertainment, local and national government, and the media industries. Intercultural negotiations form an aspect of all the contexts on the list. The prominence given to this area is significant, as students of English Language can be expected to develop skills in seeing how aspects of language and culture are at work in all contexts – for example, in teaching a group, running a business meeting, drawing up a legal document, telling a joke, making a political speech, or writing a media account of an event.

The list of areas above is not finite, so just because an area does not appear, that does not mean it is not a good context for study. The diversity of possible applications is a particular strength of English Language, in that anywhere language is used, it can be studied. That gives students plenty of options.

The list below starts with items from the benchmark statement then adds some further examples.

Education

Education is an obvious context for thinking about language because learning relies so heavily on language and communication. There is also the learning of language itself, both English (as a first, second, third language) and foreign languages.

Because education is itself such a broad area, it may be useful to divide it up into different aspects, although in practice, all the aspects are interconnected.

The environment

Educational institutions are communities that have a physical presence, suggesting their own identity. Goffman talks about the difference between 'information given', or messages produced at a conscious level, and 'information given off', or the more subtle messages we do not really know we are sending out. English Language experts can investigate both. Researching the idea of how organisations present themselves could of course include virtual identities, for example, the Wall Street Institute (Figures 5.9 and 5.10) presents its product of English tuition in a certain way in its online advertising. Researching organisational identity also does not have to be just about education or about business, you could be looking at any group that sees itself as an organisation, including charities and sports clubs.

Educational organisations will tell you a lot about themselves as soon as you enter their site, whether real or virtual. The notices, signs, logos, names and labels, documents and images that are on display are a badge of identity. These aspects lend themselves well to English Language research because language will be at the core of the communication systems referred to here.

Policies and practices

Educational organisations are shaped by government and local authority policies, which have to be put into practice by school or college managers and staff. Policies are often written documents that are points of reference for how things should work, and they help to shape the approaches taken to the different aspects of educational practice. The word 'policy' may not sound very exciting and may conjure up the idea of dusty documents sitting on a shelf, but they are the driving force behind many practical and fundamental aspects of educational life. For example, how is reading taught? How are children with special needs catered for? How are the different languages used by children in the school viewed by their teachers? What approaches are taken to regional dialect? How are experiences of different kinds of speaking and writing provided? These are just some of the questions that could be covered in a school's or college's language policy. Both the language of the policies themselves and the language outcomes they create are of interest to English Language researchers.

People and interactions

Any organisation is about its community of members and their engagement with each other; education is no exception. From the outside, a community may look like a single group of people, but in fact they are often groups of people who perform different tasks within the organisation. A school is likely to have administrators and caretakers as well as teachers; it might also have teaching assistants, staff preparing meals and supervising pupils over breaks and during exams. Each of these different groups has a particular role, which will be reflected in their language use. For example, the staff who work in the reception area might have a repertoire of styles in their interactions with all the different groups they service – pupils, teachers, parents, the head teacher, a variety of different visitors such as educational psychologists, disability workers, health and safety officers from the local council. It is important to recognise that educational establishments are more complex than being just a classroom with a teacher and pupils.

Having said that, a focus just on teachers and pupils presents a rich range of language study options, including the pupils' language skills, and aspects of teacher identity – teaching methods and styles, as well as classroom management skills.

As well as teacher–pupil interactions, there are also pupil-to-pupil, and teacher-to-teacher interactions which could reveal these groups' concerns and internal dynamics.

Resources and routines

Learning resources for language are an interesting area in their own right. The nature of different books is an obvious starting point, but there are also multimedia resources such as audio recordings and computer programmes and tools. Resources can also mean human beings – teaching assistants and disability support tutors can play an important role in children's learning experiences.

Resources can be quite closely tied to the routines, or habitual practices, that are part of the experience of learning. For example, special times and places for story reading or discussion are a frequent aspect of classroom ritual.

Discourses about education

People have views about education even though they might not actually work in the profession. This is probably because we are all 'schooled' as children, so education, like language itself, is something we experience and feel we know about. Discussions about educational issues such as standards, teaching methods, the curriculum, and the aims of learning, are frequently seen and heard in newspapers and on news programmes. Representations of education are also conveyed via 'fly on the wall' videos of classroom 'reality', and via fictions such as films and TV programmes: *To Sir with Love*, *Blackboard Jungle*, *Grange Hill*, *Hollyoaks*, *Teachers*, *Waterloo Road*, *The Wire*, *The Prime of Miss Jean Brodie*, and *Notes on a Scandal*, to name but a few.

Business

An obvious area of the business world where language features strongly is that of advertising in all its forms – paper-based, on the radio, on TV, online, and in the environment around us in the form of hoardings and electronic displays.

As well as analysing how the language of advertising tries to persuade us via these different modes and media, there are interesting differences to be observed between today's texts and those of former eras. Because advertising tries to tap into the prevailing discourses of the society that produces it, it can tell us a lot about the social aspirations of the groups it is aimed at, and about the kind of language that the copywriters saw as appropriate to address those groups.

In the online era, advertising has changed again, bringing moving print and images, colour and sound to our individual computer screens. The advertising industry uses our digital networking to help it identify who is likely to be persuaded, so that no time and effort is wasted trying to persuade the uninterested. The language of new media advertising is multimodal and interactive, sometimes imitating other genres such as quizzes and questionnaires in order to get us to respond. Meanwhile, tracking cookies are able to archive our Web trails in order to reflect back at us the browsing route we have taken, and market at us the very brands we have been viewing (Goddard and Geesin 2011).

Advertising is one aspect of business, but there are many others that are just as reliant on language. Other kinds of sales techniques have their own conversational patterns and routines, such as cold-calling on the phone and in person, and shop assistant sales talk. Staff meetings rely on language for negotiation, and organisations have to set up effective strategies for communication across different parts of the company, or even, with global companies, across different parts of the world. With English used increasingly as a **lingua franca** in intercultural communication, there are new challenges both for native speakers of English and for second language users to adapt to new international norms of English.

Members of business communities face issues of identity and power just as educators do. While trainee teachers have to learn how to perform a teacher identity, businesspeople have to do the same for their particular area of work. In both occupations, this might raise issues about how employees are seen and how their image is 'sold' to the buying public. This involves language use, either in terms of how the employees are expected to use language themselves, or else how language is used about them. For example, the badge in Figure 8.1 was a required part of the dress code for hotel workers in a Norwegian-owned Scandinavian hotel chain called 'First Hotels' during 2010. With support from the hotel workers, English guests complained to

Figure 8.1 *Sleep with us*: a badge worn by employees of a Norwegian chain hotel

the company, after which the badge was removed. 'Sleep with us' was not a mistranslation, as other pieces of advertising in the hotel literature featured images of businessmen being served by sexy models dressed as French maids.

Media representations of business worlds abound, as reality TV genres (*Mary Queen of Shops*, *The Apprentice*, *The Business Inspector*, *Dragon's Den*, *The Secret Millionaire*), as TV comedy and satire (*The Office*, *Only Fools and Horses*, *Open All Hours*, *Mad Men*), as films (*Working Girl*, *Up in the Air*) and plays (*Death of a Salesman*, *Top Girls*).

A further area of representation can be seen in 'airport literature' which markets the idea of business success via advice from supposed experts. The titles of these texts are often very specific, such as *The 7 Habits of Highly Effective People* (Covey 1989) and *If Life is a Game, These Are the Rules: 10 Rules for Being Human* (Carter Scott 1999) constructing the business world as a matter of personal psychology. Thurlow and Jaworski (2006) researched an allied kind of literature, in the form of airline marketing to business class travellers. They call this discourse 'the alchemy of the upwardly mobile', seeing the marketing as offering elusive and impossible dreamworlds.

Law

This area of application offers many opportunities for English Language experts to focus on register, or field-specific language use. This is because legal contexts often rely on pre-agreed meanings for items of language within fixed written genres such as house conveyancing documents, sales contracts, wills, and so on. In some cases, if there is variation in language use, then the legality of the transaction can be questioned. This can apply to those professional groups who are not themselves lawyers, but who play a specific part in a legal process – for example, the police, who have to caution people they arrest by going through a set form of words, or registrars conducting wedding ceremonies in registry offices. In courts, there are ritual forms of language that are strictly adhered to, like swearing oaths, and also conventionalised professional practices, such as how to cross-examine witnesses.

The courts, like Parliament, are very ritualised in terms of dress and actions, and so there is scope for looking at the part played by the language of dress in signalling power hierarchies, and also the rules about where people stand and sit. Terms of address also carry great significance, with some terms that would be considered antique in everyday life functioning to establish social position and what Goffman (1963) termed 'the interaction order' – who has speaking rights and when and where (and how) they can exercise them.

A particular area of language expertise that has grown considerably in recent years is that of forensic linguistics. Forensics in general is the application of scientific methods to legal problems and issues, such as whether a set of documents has a consistent style of authorship, or where a speaker might be from, in questions of identity. Forensic linguists can be involved in quite high profile cases and can be asked to analyse contemporary, everyday communications such as txt messages. One case that received a lot of media attention was that of Stuart Campbell, who was convicted in 2002 of murdering his niece. What helped to convict him was forensic linguistics evidence showing that the murder victim's style of txting had changed after she disappeared. Campbell had sent messages to himself from his niece's phone in order to give himself an alibi, but had spelt 'what' as 'wot', while the girl had consistently used 'wat' in her previous messages ('Text messages examined in Danielle case', BBC News) http://news.bbc.co.uk/1/hi/england/2478639.stm.

Forensic linguists are not the white-coated lab techs of *CSI*, but experts in areas of language use such as phonetics, dialectology, and discourse analysis. Many work at universities and their analyses have to be painstaking, but the techniques they use can certainly be studied at more basic levels and are similar to the kinds of activities that are part of degree programmes. In fact, you could call many past and current activities people have engaged in, in their everyday lives, 'forensic'. If you have ever had a message from someone which has seemed 'out of character', if you have ever suspected that someone on a website was not who they claimed (termed 'trolling'), if you have ever speculated whether a piece of writing was plagiarised, then you have already used your skills in forensic linguistics. Literary critics who argued about whether Shakespeare was the author of all of the plays ascribed to him, and new media critics who spotted a well-known historian giving his own book a rave review and blasting invective at a rival, were also doing forensic linguistics of a certain kind.

There is clearly a lot more that could be said about the language of legal contexts, including all the aspects of interaction between professionals and the general public, and all the documents that are part of legal processes. You can see that there are many interesting areas for English Language researchers to delve into.

Representations of legal figures are also too numerous to mention in detail – think of all the books, TV programmes, and films that feature crime and punishment, including the whole area of prison culture. And there are less high-profile types of representation, too, such as police recruitment literature, notes from local police forces sent to households about particular issues and events, and debates about the legal system in the media.

Performance arts

If Goffman's idea of everyday life as a performance (see Chapter 4) is right, then we are all performing in one way or another. But some people get others to pay them for doing this, and it counts as a professional activity. What are they doing, then, that allows them to call their behaviour 'art' and gets us to open our wallets?

You could include literary fiction here, and this would certainly feature as a strong context for the application of English Language concepts and ideas. But much has already been said about this area, as part of the subject coverage in Chapters 4–7, so there is no need to repeat that information here. However, drama and performance poetry have not been mentioned, nor have other aspects of artistic performance such as stand-up comedy, street theatre acts or busking.

Performance arts feature on academic courses, and tend to be classified into drama, dance and music (art in the sense of drawing is often classified as 'fine art', not as performance). Each of these areas has its own kind of discourse, both in terms of academic views of the work produced, and also the type of discourse associated with individual performance events or products. So, to take music as an example, there are academic articles about different types of music, there is music journalism (music magazines, music reviews in newspapers), there are music flyers and programmes surrounding performances, and there are the musical products themselves in a variety of formats. All of these discourses involve language use, so there are many possible applications here.

A focus more on the 'performance' aspect of performing arts is also possible. Drama and poetry have written versions of their art, but are also performed. Looking at the differences wrought by mode gets at the different communication potentials of spoken and written language, which is an important area for English Language students to think about.

Stand-up comedy is different again, as for some performers it appears to incorporate a level of spontaneity both in the themes covered and in interaction with the audience. But whatever their style, and however funny or unfunny you think they are, the strategies they use for humour are worth studying; and many performances are now on YouTube, so there is access to a lot of material.

Humour in general – not just stand-up comedy – is a great area for thinking about different cultural norms, including all the aspects of social group identity and representation that have been discussed already. Humour often involves language play, and can be found in many contexts, from newspaper cartoons through birthday cards to messages sent in to radio shows by the public. Witty examples of the latter occur frequently, but a memorable extended episode unfolded on the wedding day of the now Duke and Duchess of Cambridge on 29 April 2011, when broadcasters Nicky Campbell and Shelagh Fogerty on BBC's *Five Live* Breakfast Show invited listeners to 'invent' their own aristocratic name for the occasion. The way to do this was:

- choose 'lady' or 'lord' as your title, according to your sex;
- choose your grandmother's or grandfather's first name, as appropriate to your sex;
- add the name of your very first pet;
- finish with the name of a street or road where you've lived.

A wonderful list of bizarre and eccentric-sounding names flooded in – 'Lady Nellie Pinky Pellhurst' was one. Bound up with the wordgame, of course, was satire aimed at the aristocracy – something that seemed entirely fitting on the day of a UK royal event.

You may disagree with the statement above, considering that it was disrespectful to be making jokes about such high-level figures. If so, you've revealed another aspect of language and humour, which is about **taboo,** or areas that are culturally off-limits and so not to be aired either in speech or writing. Humour often pushes the boundaries of taboo in addressing areas that have complex cultural histories attached to them, so in pointing out aspects of language you are also quarrying deep into a society's attitudes and values.

Politics

The times when politicians are particularly noticeable are when they are making speeches at, for example, their party conferences and during election periods. You could say that speeches are a performance art in themselves, and many of the discourse-analytic aspects you might look at in analysing stand-up comedy routines – timing, repetition, patterning of sounds and/or lexical items, metaphor, interactive features, non-verbal behaviour – could serve you well in approaching political speech-making. The classical study of **rhetoric**, or strategies for oral persuasion, has a long tradition and offers many language-based **tropes** or techniques as part of its analytical toolkit.

There are many further contexts for studying political discourse, ranging from the ritualised (parliamentary debates) to the freewheeling (radio phone-ins) and from speech (speeches, press conferences, committee hearings) to writing (campaign leaflets, drafts of legislation, letters to and from MPs) to multimodal communication (computer-based discussion forums and chat, the use of social media, electronic mail-outs to party members).

Representations of politics and politicians have a long history, both in terms of covering actual events, such as the Watergate scandal in America (*All the President's Men*) or President Kennedy's assassination (*JFK*), and fictional depictions of political life (*Yes, Prime Minister*, *The Thick of It*). Moving away from individual political figures and politics as a professional career, political viewpoints are also, of course expressed routinely by the mass media outlets in any society and can be studied in a range of media formats.

Media

The media have been referred to many times in this chapter as useful sources to use for exploration of different topics. But they have not been discussed as organisations that themselves employ professionals who can be studied. The latter is an interesting option for English Language researchers, not least because new media have radically changed the way journalists do their jobs and the nature of their language use.

The development of Web 2.0 has radically altered the relationship between media professionals and the public. At the core of Web 2.0 technology is the ability it gives ordinary individuals to create their own content, not just read officially published material. This means not only that there are many more 'citizen journalists' – local people giving their own version of events for free – but also that professional journalists have many more sources of information they can tap into, with social media offering them details they might have had to work hard to discover. For example, in July 2011, a right-wing Norwegian extremist bombed Oslo then shot many young people at a summer camp nearby. As the story developed, TV news outlets rapidly acquired images of the perpetrator from his Facebook pages, where he had 'published' his own manifesto for his attack. Such immediate access to the personal details of individuals has not been possible in the past. The amount of information available from so many different electronic sources such as Twitter, blogs, and social media means that a lot of journalism is about sorting, sifting and compiling information. Those sources are also globally available as never before. During the popular uprisings across the Middle East in 2011, citizen journalists regularly captured images that were relayed by Western media when the professional journalists were not allowed in the countries.

Sports journalism is an interesting case study of how the different new media have radically changed the language conventions of reporting. The phenomenon of 'live text', for example, which offers frequently updated web information to describe live sports fixtures such as football, relies on official observers at matches phoning in to a central news point to relay descriptions of events, which are then adapted to a text-style format and added to the respective webpage. The resulting language has formulaic expressions and set conventions for colour, such as black bars for goals. Presumably, this convention allows readers to register key events where the screen is very small, as on mobile devices, or a long way away, as on a TV screen in a bar or gym. Live text pages also now incorporate comments from a wide range of sources, including members of the public, so that any page could have a mixture of match-related narrative accounts and discursive posts that are more interactive and dialogic.

While new communication systems have changed the way journalists produce their texts, the same systems have changed the way many news consumers get their news. As well as the news feeds available from internet service providers, there are now online versions of most newspapers, so newspapers themselves are offering more than one version of the same story. These different formats are interesting territory for English Language study, as digital text is so differently organised from paper-based versions, offering a very different kind of reading experience, as well as providing archived editions that were previously only available on microfiche from libraries.

Despite the proliferation of formats, media products can still be analysed to reveal their particular ideologies – magazines and advertising, as well as newspapers. There are now electronic versions of the former, of course, with their own new language strategies for the electronic age.

More applications ...

There are many more potential applications for interdisciplinary English Language study than this chapter has room to cover. A brief mention of a few further areas is all that is possible:

- *Computer worlds*. Fantasy environments offer opportunities to study language use in artificially created worlds. There are also many everyday human–computer interactions where programmed routines can be observed working, or not.

- *Counselling and therapy*. Counselling involve interactions where therapists often have specific aims and procedures that they try to follow. Some approaches, for example, cognitive behavioural therapy, are particularly about language and thinking.
- *Science and medicine*. There continue to be attempts to popularise science and make its discourses more accessible. A range of texts – from TV programmes to health leaflets and books for children – could show these processes in action.
- *Theolinguistics*. This area focuses on language and faith, considering the role of language in theological practices and texts.

9

Research methods for English Language

Undertaking a piece of independent research is an expected part of many English Language degrees, as it is of many school-based English Language specifications.

At degree level, there may also be modules explicitly addressing the nature of different research methods, as a single topic can be researched in many different ways.

Research methods come from the academic areas where they were devised, so it is logical that because English Language draws on a number of fields, that a range of different methods is available. It is also the case that academic research often uses mixed methods, so there is no obligation to stick completely to one method throughout.

Benchmark statements

The benchmark statements say the following about the skills that English Language courses should promote in their students:

- awareness of the structure and use of geographical, social, and historical varieties of English;
- skills shared with General Linguistics in data collection and analysis;
- critical skills shared with Literature and Media Studies in how discourses represent the world around us;
- awareness shared with Creative Writing courses of the implications of

> language choices and of the cultural, literary and historical context in
> which the texts were produced.

This means that the research that students do can range widely across the areas mentioned above, that there is no narrow definition of boundaries for English Language study. That's very good news from a research perspective.

What is data?

The statements above refer to data collection and analysis, and skills that are shared with General Linguistics. This academic area has often taken an **empirical** approach to research, which is all about observation and sometimes about testing and experimentation. Empiricism has come from scientific fields and in English Language study it may be appropriate to test out an idea or **hypothesis** in a scientific way, for example, testing out participants' reaction times or responses in order to gain a better understanding of how language is processed in our brains. An empirical approach tends to use the language of science to describe its activities – you would probably talk about your 'data' and your 'findings' or 'results' in a similar way to laboratory-based scientists.

The term 'observation' as used in science refers to the researcher noticing effects that can be pointed out and shown. This approach can also be described as **positivistic.** Positivism is all about things observably happening. The idea of data in this case would be the evidence of your observation or experimentation.

There are many areas of Linguistics that are not scientific in the laboratory sense of the word. However, they may still use the general ideas of empirical research and also its associated language, like 'hypothesis'. The social sciences of Sociology and Psychology both have strands of empirical work, from which Sociolinguistics and Psycholinguistics have borrowed some approaches. For example, variationist studies of accent and dialect in Sociolinguistics look at ways to identify linguistic variables, or the items of language that might vary between different populations. The idea of holding some things constant while observing whether an identified element changes, is taken from scientific contexts of experimentation.

But it is possible to take another view of empirical evidence, and the idea of observation. The **critical** skills referred to in the statements above come from a different philosophical and sociological tradition and are seen more in Literary, Media Studies and other related fields (such as Cultural Studies).

Creative Writing can also be associated with ideas of criticality because criticality is seen as an important accompaniment to creative outputs.

Criticality refers to the activity of critiquing, which is to question the concepts that underlie society, including approaches to research. No approach to research is seen as natural or neutral, so critical theories would question the whole idea of observation as just 'seeing what is there'. Observation, from a critical theory perspective, involves a viewer and therefore as we saw in Chapter 5, a point of view. Critical theory researchers stress the presence of the researcher and include the researcher in the picture rather than trying to make him or her disappear from view. This level of explicit self-reflection is associated with postmodern approaches to research in all academic fields, which questions whether there is any such thing as objective truth.

Rather than trying to understand all the complexities of different theories and academic fields, there are some key points to grasp for English Language research. The first is that research does not have to be experimental or based on a notion of testing. Following on from this, data does not have to be what is produced by experimentation, or the pursuit of variables, or the result of having a hypothesis. If your interests lie in aspects of language and culture, for example, your data can be what you collect in order to explore cultural concepts and practices, and the research that follows can incorporate the researcher's position. There is no merit in notions of 'objectivity' if there is no such thing as objective truth. And subjectivity can be seen very positively as telling the truth about the researcher's views and position, leading to a more reliable story because at least you know who is telling it. Critical-theoretical approaches can also depart from the language of science in telling the research story, so 'findings' and 'results' might simply be 'analysis' or 'arguments'.

Data for English Language study can therefore consist of many different kinds of material – it depends what you are trying to find out. In Chapter 5 we saw that the terms 'text' and 'discourse' can refer to whole stretches of written and spoken language, and even the social codes of dress and behaviour that work alongside verbal language to make meaning. Data can be as small as a speech noise or as big as a building: Deborah Schiffrin (1987) studied how people use 'Oh' in their spoken interactions, in order to understand more about how discourse markers work; John Swales (1998) conducted a 'textography', looking at all the genres of written communication that were on display inside a university building, in order to show how the building could be 'read' or seen as expressing an identity. The data you collect should be connected with your research aim, but it is also important to recognise that interpretation, and not simply observation, is likely to be needed, especially if you are researching language and culture. Clifford Geertz, an influential figure in research on meaning in cultural contexts, used a metaphor of the spider's web to offer his perspective on what he was seeking to explain and where he was looking for his data:

> The concept of culture I espouse ... is essentially a semiotic one. Believing, with Max Weber, that humans are animals suspended in webs of significance they themselves have spun, I take culture to be those webs, and the analysis of it to be therefore not an experimental science in search of law but an interpretive one in search of meaning.
>
> (Geertz 1973: 5)

Discussion of theories and approaches at this level is a challenging task, and you will not necessarily be expected to be this explicit in explaining what you are doing. However, it is important to understand different traditions, particularly since their research methods and also the language that they use to express their ideas are different. If students can understand why different sorts of language are coming at them, it is less confusing for them. In addition, if they can explain why they are approaching their research task in a certain way, rather than just following the approach of a particular researcher, then they will be seen as operating at a high standard.

What is a research question?

At the most basic level, a research question expresses the aim of the research work – what is the researcher trying to find out?

Working out a research question, and therefore a research plan, involves a lot of thought, and takes time. It is also useful to talk ideas through: articulating ideas aloud helps the thinking process. Any researcher at any level needs their research to be:

- *Interesting to them.* It's important not to be thrown off track by others' opinions of whether an area is interesting or not. Everyone has different interests and motivations for what they do, and it's vital to do something that generates a sense of personal engagement. Doing something idiosyncratic is not a problem – unless it is unrealistic (see below). At the same time, there is no problem in tackling an area that many others have tried, since the way any one individual does research, including the data they gather, will make their research original.

- *Realistic and achievable.* We all want to know the answer to the big questions in life, but good research is often modest in its aims and does not try to do too much. It is important for researchers to say what they are *not* aiming to do as well as explaining what they are. Research needs a sharp focus on the topic concerned (what exactly it is) and an appropriate scope (how many dimensions of it are being covered). Thinking about available resources is important. It is no good aiming to study something where it will be impossible (or dangerous, or unethical) to get data.
- *Ethical and sensitive.* All research has an effect on the world in some way, but particularly so if it involves human subjects. Behaving ethically means ensuring that permission is given to research a chosen person or group (or if not, that their refusal is accepted without any consequences to them), and that people are offered the chance to withdraw if they become unhappy about the direction the research is taking. Research should not name anyone or give any information that makes them locatable. It should also not harm them in any way, for example, by making them anxious or feeling like they have failed. There is usually some documentation that is provided by course leaders to ensure that research plans are ethically framed, and where the agreement of participants can be recorded.

Sensitivity is also required by researchers to the position they are in, particularly how they might be seen by any individual or organisation that is the subject of research. For example, a school might feel that their practices are being 'inspected' and that any research findings will get into the public domain. It is important to think about ways to make the research activity of value to the people being researched, as well as to the researcher.

But the question remains – how can a research question be identified, among all the wide choices available? Here are some possible starting points:

- *Taught courses.* Many people pick up a research interest from courses they have already studied and where an aspect was covered briefly that intrigued them, so they wanted to learn more.
- *Personal experiences.* Researching an aspect of language that has played a part in your life can be very rewarding and lead to some excellent research because you have some personal experience. You may have understood the issue or aspect from the inside, as it were, but this gives you a chance to view it a bit more dispassionately.
- *Things that are puzzling.* Research is about looking more deeply in order to explain how things work, so it can address the puzzling nature of some aspects of language use and attitudes, for example.

- *Things that are amazing, amusing, annoying.* Tapping into one's own reactions to language can be a useful starting point because, like the feeling of puzzlement, it gives the researcher a question to answer – why am I amazed/amused/annoyed?

- *Things that tie in with future plans.* If you have a particular career in mind or simply a general area of work, then research on a relevant area can be very useful practically as well as interesting.

- *Things that are possible.* This is a repeat of the 'realistic and achievable' idea, from the previous bulleted list. No apologies for repeating this point, because it is very important and a common cause of the early failure of research plans. What people and materials are accessible? Are there some immediate contexts of involvement, such as different groups or workplaces or activities, that could generate questions and data? Think about what is around on the ground before reaching for the skies.

- *Things that will develop skills.* People know their strengths and weaknesses and although research can open up new abilities that you never knew you had, it's no good choosing to study an area if it's going to involve working on an aspect of language where you are unlikely to improve and that you don't really enjoy. Use the opportunity to sharpen the skills you would like to take to the next level.

What is a 'literature review'?

Whatever the starting point, doing research involves looking at what others have said about a chosen area. Writing an account of what others have said is termed a 'literature review'. A review is not a list of books with a paragraph of description or 'blurb' after each. It is more like an essay on the ideas involved in researching a topic, with academic articles, books, and any other sources brought into the discussion. Sources need to be referenced properly: referencing conventions should be made clear at the beginning of courses and/or before assignments.

The aim of a literature review is not to claim that the researcher is the only person ever to think of researching a chosen topic, but to show that they know about others who have looked at this area and what they have found. Sometimes researchers justifiably claim they are filling in some areas that have been missed, or focusing in more detail on something. Whatever the claims being made, by the end of the review there should have been an explanation of how the area has been researched and what has been concluded. It may be that you use similar methods to do your investigation, or you may feel that you want to disagree with other approaches and use a new method, or a mixture of approaches.

What is a research method?

The simple answer to this question is that a research method is a rationale for collecting and analysing data. Obviously, any method should be strongly connected with the research aim – it should be a way of carrying out the research question.

There are many different methods, but a distinction is often made between **qualitative** and **quantitative** methods. Most of the methods used in the research reported in this book are qualitative – that is, attempting to explain the nature of language by looking in detail at specific contexts of use. Qualitative research is often rich in detail, but its weakness is that it is harder to generalise its findings across lots of different contexts. However, it is often claimed by qualitative researchers that trying to make universal statements is not appropriate anyway.

Quantitative research bases its findings on numerical factors, as the term itself suggests. Statistical methods are often used to analyse quantitative data, with different parts of the data or different populations compared statistically. Examples of quantitative research can be seen in large-scale analyses of accent features, such as those done by Trudgill (1978) on populations in Norwich. In more recent times, large **corpora** of language have been collected and stored on computers, then analysed statistically for particular features of language. The best-known collection is the British National Corpus (BNC), a collection of 100 million words of spoken and written English, but there are many others; and some universities are developing their own corpora that reflect local language use or particular interests.

There is no problem with combining qualitative and quantitative methods, as each approach can both contribute some understanding to a research question.

As a way to illustrate some different research methods, the rest of this section will focus primarily on the possible applications of English Language research to education, as was outlined in Chapter 8. The same headings will be used here, in order to think about different aspects of educational contexts.

Before discussing any research approaches, it should be emphasised that researching any community must be done with the full co-operation of its members. It is assumed here that any researcher would have planned their research with the school's managers, and that anything undertaken would be seen as beneficial to the development of the school. Also it is assumed that any legal requirements – for example, Criminal Records Bureau (CRB) checks – would have been done.

The environment

Research that aims to analyse the environment of educational communities might look at particular aspects of their physical organisation and focus on the possible meanings conveyed, for example, the messages given about the school or college by the look of the entrance area, with all its signs and symbols, documents, posters, and so on. This would lend itself to a semiotic approach, and a way to collect data would be to take photographs or, if there was an interest in how people use the space, to do some video recording. Scollon and Scollon (2003) talk of the importance of 'discourses in place', by which they mean that a significant aspect of meaning is often conveyed by where messages appear, not just what they say in terms of their words. A good example of this idea is the message given by where children's work is placed, on school walls: if it's at adult height, then its audience is clearly not the children themselves.

Goffman's (1963) work on behaviour in public places and his ideas about how people perform their identities (Goffman 1969) are still relevant to researchers looking at the public, socially oriented nature of human behaviour, particularly how people organise themselves. Fox (2005) focuses on behaviour that she sees as embedded in English cultural rules.

Educational environments are not only physical, they can also be virtual; and this brings new dimensions of communication into play. Semiotic approaches could also encompass the way schools and colleges market themselves online. If the question was more about how students use the virtual learning environment, however, there would need to be more of a focus on how participants present themselves (Chandler 2006) and manage different genres of 'e-language' (Goddard and Geesin 2011).

The ideas here could be applied to the environment of any community, not just educational ones.

Policies and practices

Analysing the policies that underlie the way communities organise themselves is a task of text analysis, and the approaches to point of view and other aspects of narrative outlined in Chapter 5 would be relevant here. An English Language study might focus on some specific aspects that relate to language, such as the school's language policy, which might include its position on regional language, on multilingualism and multiculturalism, on disability, and on supporting literacy and oracy.

If you (and the school) were interested in seeing how aspects of the policy were put into practice, then a different method would need to be adopted to research the practical effects. You could construct a questionnaire for the teaching staff to answer, and/or research their experiences and perspectives via a focus group or semi-structured interviews; if you were focusing on a specific aspect that could be followed through to pupils' activities, for example, approaches to reading, you could participate in reading activities and see for yourself the relationship between policy and practice. Sometimes this type of follow-up, looking at how policies influence work on the ground, is termed 'action research'.

People and interactions

The nature and position of different groups within a community will be reflected in their repertoires of language use. To study this would be a sociolinguistic enterprise because it would involve the relationship between their language and their social role.

In a study of the language of London schoolchildren, Rampton (2002) recorded groups of children, using lapel microphones, for hours at a time, learning much about the identities they performed from moment to moment within their groups, and also about the way they used the language of their different lessons as a resource for gaining social power in interactions. A study of this scale takes a considerable amount of time, money, organisation and expertise, but you can study participant identities on a much smaller scale by observing and recording particular episodes.

The data below is from an English Language student's recording of a secondary school English lesson, where the teacher is studying a poem called 'The Fog' by F.R. McCreary with pupils. Here is the poem:

The Fog

Slowly, the fog,
Hunch-shouldered with a grey face,
Arms wide, advances,

Finger tips touching the way
Past the dark houses
And dark gardens of roses.
Up the short street from the harbour,
Slowly the fog,
Seeking, seeking;
Arms wide, shoulders hunched,
Searching, searching.
Out through the streets to the fields,
Slowly, the fog –
A blind man hunting the moon.

(F. R. McCreary)

And here is the classroom discussion the teacher had with the pupils about the poem:

[square brackets indicate actions]
/forward slashes indicate intonation boundaries:

Teacher
Pupils = Joanne, James, Frances

Teacher: Frances/stand up/read out loud/
[Pupil reads poem]

Teacher: good/right/sit down
[Teacher repeats the reading of the poem]

Teacher:	right/Joanne/why does the fog/move slowly/why slowly/go on
Joanne:	um
Teacher:	well/what does slowly mean
Joanne:	um
Teacher:	why does the fog/move slowly
James:	because
Teacher:	go on/James
James:	um
Teacher:	why slowly/why not quickly
James:	because fog moves slow

Teacher: because fog moves slowly/right/tell me/what does fog do/ Frances/what does fog do/to things

Frances: makes things/like/almost invisible

Teacher: makes things invisible/good/then why do we say/hunch shouldered/what does that mean/if you see something/ hunch shouldered/what does that mean/ok/what does that mean/Frances

Frances: hugged up/snugged up/ready to strike

Teacher: ready to strike/that's good/why is it

Frances: well/cats always do/like hunch up/when they're going to pounce

Teacher: good/good/a man called Eliot/wrote a poem/about fog/ and he described it/as a cat being hunch shouldered/good/ why then hunched/what does it mean/what does hunch shouldered/what kind of vision does it make/what kind of picture/does it make/in your mind

This interaction can be analysed from a number of perspectives. It shows a particular kind of subject-based discourse, and if your focus was on how pupils learn the language of different subject areas, you would be talking about the type of discourse referred to in Chapter 5, as ways of thinking, talking, writing, about a subject. In this case, the discourse is that of a certain kind of literary criticism. When the teacher asks 'why does the fog move slowly?' she is not asking a question about physics or meteorology, it is a question about the poet's choice of language and imagery. The real question (the pragmatics of the utterance) is 'why did the poet describe the fog as moving slowly?' The pupils struggle to understand what she is asking, but James' rather obvious-seeming answer 'because fog moves slowly' is responded to with approval because the question is about the relationship between the poetic imagery and real-life fog. Frances 'gets' the discourse more readily in her elaboration of 'hunch shouldered'.

Another aspect of the interaction to focus on could be the language strategies employed by the teacher to manage the pupils and to claim her role and status as 'teacher'. This would be more of an interactional sociolinguistic approach (see Chapter 4) because the focus would be on language and social role. Her own reading of the poem, and her naming of individual pupils, putting them 'on the spot', are part of her management of the group. But she is also very encouraging, using a familiar routine in classroom discourse of three-part exchanges (see Coulthard and Brazil 1992): teacher asks a question, pupil answers, teacher responds, in this case with approval.

These two ideas – of types of discourse, and of the social roles of participants in interactions – can be applied to the study of any community.

Resources and routines

The poem being discussed could simply have been read silently by each pupil, working on their own. But the teacher chose to have it read aloud, and then she repeated the reading. 'Reading aloud' is a convention or routine of school English lessons, symbolising the idea of a shared experience of literature, particularly poetry.

These types of unspoken conventions are at work in any community and suggest the idea of scripting and schemas that were discussed in Chapter 4. The rules for organising talk – for example, who has speaking rights, how turn-taking is managed – are also of interest in conversation analysis (Sacks 1995) as evidence of how people construct their social interactions.

The poem was set as part of an anthology for GCSE, and so constitutes a 'resource' in the educational context. Written resources are an interesting aspect of any community because they construct, as well as reflect, the values of the members or those who are in ultimate control of the group. The teacher might have had some choices within the anthology, but would have been obliged to teach it as part of the assessment process at GCSE. To that extent, the resources available to her have already constructed her world, and that of her pupils. Looking at curricula and resources can lead to many interesting questions about the politics of language use as discussed in Chapter 4.

Resources can construct points of view even when they do not appear to be telling a story. The discussion of narrative in Chapter 5 highlighted some of the ways in which any text must have a standpoint, and this can be explored with reference to whose world is represented in the resources of the classroom (or any other community).

An example of a narrative that often passes unnoticed involves the figures who populate language-teaching books. There are many such texts that aim to teach foreign languages, but there are also books that focus not so much on teaching how to speak a language, but how to analyse it. For example, Palmer's (1984) *Grammar*, was aimed at readers who wanted to increase their structural knowledge of English. It was a popular book of its time, featuring on many academic reading lists.

Language textbooks such as Palmer's often contain examples of sentences for the writer to analyse in order to illustrate a point. Such examples are probably considered by the writers as of no importance and no meaning, but actually they still describe a world. Palmer's book has a couple, John and Mary, who are characterised in particular ways in the invented examples of language that are used. John is a well-meaning soul, harried along by a nagging but scatterbrained wife. Palmer invents some dialogue in order to illustrate what he considers to be the nature of everyday speech:

MARY: John! Coming?
JOHN: Yes dear, I was only -
MARY: Oh do hurry up and - we ought to catch the bus - only they don't always run on time - wretched people - as long as you're quick. I've been ready for some - since half past seven.

(Palmer 1984)

Having made up the dialogue, Palmer claims typicality for this text: 'Such a conversation is not abnormal; much of our everyday speech is like this' (ibid.: 67).

Throughout the textbook, there are 122 invented examples of utterances involving male and female figures as the grammatical subjects in active sentences. Of these, 112 are male and 10 are female. The verbs that **collocate** frequently with the male subjects are 'hit', 'make', 'give', 'meet' and 'see', with sentences often reflecting dynamic activities, either in a physical sense or in terms of social and professional work, for example:

He hit a man bigger than me
John made Bill president

On the other hand, verbs that follow the female subjects often place women in traditional domestic roles, or characterise them as fanciful or inadequate, for example:

She washed the fabric
She made up the whole story
She only passed French

Where male and female figures are in the same sentence, the male figure is almost invariably the subject and the female the **object**, for example:

The boy hit the girl with a stick

The young man followed the girl

A fair bit of detail has been presented here in order to indicate the work involved in researching language and representation – here, of gender. This analysis focuses on grammar, because that is what the book's topic is, and so that determines Palmer's examples. But representation can come in many forms: in a child's picture book, the images may need particular attention.

If your research question concerns how worlds are represented in the written resources that are aimed at, or represent, a particular group, you may need to give some extra thought to the scope of your project. Trying to analyse whole texts is a time-consuming task, and can be overwhelming. The process of selection is important, and can be based on a straightforward premise, such as the selection of the contents page of a magazine as a 'shopfront' of the whole text's ideology (McLoughlin 2000), or one specific story covered in a range of news outlets, or the choice of a book on the basis of its popularity, or some advertising of a specific type of product. Media texts are readily available, but that in itself presents a challenge for selection.

Discourses about education

Representations of education could involve the analysis of many different types of text, from films and TV programmes, to books and newspapers. Again, the task of analysis is made considerably easier if the selection process has been carefully thought through. Analysing a whole film or TV programme is only likely to be achievable if a specific focus is defined, for example, how a particular character is constructed through language, or how teacher–pupil interactions are fictionalised. Analysing literary texts is a stylistics task, while looking at how educational issues are reported in the media will need to connect language and representation with the ideologies of the media organisations. The educational issue being covered will have a history of representation, so there may be useful articles to explore in books and journals about teaching and learning. Particular attitudes to language in education may also connect with attitudes to language elsewhere. For example, attitudes to children's use of new technologies can be seen to connect with public attitudes to language change (Goddard and Geesin 2011).

10

Careers for students of English Language

Chapter 9 showed how many different research options can be generated from a single context, and suggested the value of focusing on a context that might be a future workplace.

Benchmark statement

The English Language benchmark document is at pains to point out the strong links that can be made between the subject and aspects of work environments:

> Language issues are present in every workplace and can be meaningfully studied towards an outcome beneficial to employers as well as to the students themselves and their programmes.

The document also identifies particular skills developed by English Language courses, and links these with examples of occupational areas:
English Language provides a grounding for careers requiring:

- advanced written and spoken communication skills, such as management, the media, publishing;
- skills in processing information, such as journalism, the law;
- subject-specific knowledge, such as teaching, language therapy, forensic linguistics.

You may be at a very early stage in deciding where your interests lie, but knowing about the employment directions others have taken before you is no bad thing. Every year, the Higher Education Statistics Agency (HESA) produces information about graduate career paths as a result of conducting surveys with students six months after they have graduated. This information is then turned into an annual report called *What do Graduates Do?: Career Planning for Higher Education and Beyond*. The latest information available at the time of writing covers those who graduated in 2009, and there are links in the Further Reading and Resources chapter which will take you both to this report and to the graduate careers site, *Prospects*, that houses the annual data. Each year, the document provides a snapshot which offers some useful insights, but you need to remember that six months is not very long and it is often the case that graduates take longer than that to settle into their chosen long-term career.

Nevertheless, here are some facts and figures that should tell you a little about the career orientations of the subject community. The statistics do not separate the different parts of English study. This is their list of the disciplines covered by the general subject heading of 'English' in the report:

> English Language
> English as a second language
> English Literature
> English Studies

A separate part of the same report covers languages, so if you are studying English Language alongside other languages, you could look at that section as well. It is not reproduced here, but can be found by following the links mentioned previously. If you want to compare the figures for employment of English Language graduates with those from other subject areas, you can also find those in the same report.

Data from the 2009 English graduates was as shown in Table 10.1. Examples of further study include: Linguistics, Marketing, Journalism, Business Management, Acting, Creative Writing and Law.

The 2009 graduates were employed in a wide range of occupations. The report offers some real examples of jobs attained in some of the categories, which helps to give a sense of what the headings refer to (Table 10.2).

This information might help to generate some ideas about the types of workplace that you could target for possible placements and future careers. It illustrates just how varied a range of careers English students go into.

Table 10.1 **Statistics on recent graduates, 2009**

	Total	Percentage
All graduates	10,535	
Responses received	8,545	
Response rate		81.1
Female	6,345	
Male	2,200	
In UK employment		49.9
In employment abroad		2
Working and studying		8.3
Studying in the UK for a higher degree		10.7
Studying in the UK for a teaching qualification: (English, Drama, Media)		5.8
Other further study or training in the UK		5
Other further study or training abroad		0.3
Believed to be unemployed		9
Not available for employment, study of training		4.3
Other		4.7

Table 10.2 **Graduate job examples, 2009**

Heading	Job title	Percentage
Marketing, Sales and Advertising Professionals	Advertising Sales Co-ordinator at ITV	7
	Press officer for the Department of Work and Pensions	
	Marketing assistant for a football club	
Commercial, Industrial and Public Sector Managers	Graduate trainee at John Lewis	7.9
Scientific Research, Analysis and Development Professionals	Market researcher for FDS company	0.1
	Researcher at the Royal Bank of Scotland (RBS)	
Engineering Professionals		0.2
Health Professionals		0.5

(continued)

Table 10.2 **Graduate job examples, 2009** *(continued)*

Heading	Job title	Percentage
Education Professionals (e.g. primary/secondary school teachers)		9.3
Business and Financial Professionals	Fraud prevention officer at RBS	5.2
	Management trainee at HSBC	
	Accountant with KPMG	
Information Technology Professionals	IT analyst for O2	0.8
Arts, Design, Culture and Sports Professionals	Assistant editor for a publisher	6.6
	Media intern at a national newspaper	
	Gallery assistant at a national gallery	
	Production assistant at the BBC	
Legal Professionals	Witness liaison officer for the Crown Prosecution Service	0.3
Social and Welfare Professionals		4.3
Other Professionals	Policy intern in Brussels	2
	HR adviser for Lloyds TSB	
Numerical clerks and cashiers		1.9
Other Clerical and Secretarial Occupations	Music administrator at ITV	15.1
Retail, Catering, Waiting and Bar Staff	Visual merchandiser for New Look	23
Other Occupations	Officer in the Royal Marines	15.9
Unknown occupations		0.1

While English is not an applied area in the sense of veterinary science or architecture, its graduates acquire high level communication skills which are valued in many professions. Chapter 11 focuses on what skills employers say they want to see in graduate applicants, and offer some starting points for thinking about how to match those requirements with your own developing expertise.

11

Building a CV

CV stands for curriculum vitae, which is Latin for 'your life's course'. There are many guides to CV writing, including services that will be offered by careers staff in educational organisations. This chapter, then, is not a CV writing manual in any step-by-step way, but rather a guide on how to identify the skills that are typically acquired through the study of English Language. Detailing the facts and figures of your history and achievements – the factual bit of a CV – is one thing. But the more difficult task is to talk about, not where you have studied and worked, or what you have done, but the skills you have acquired and the abilities you have.

What do employers want?

The report on graduate destinations referred to in Chapter 10 identifies four broad areas of skill that employers say they are looking for in taking on new employees. These skills are listed below, with some questions to ask yourself about your study experiences. If you are just embarking on a degree programme, you will probably be given advice on how to record and articulate your development – sometimes this is called a 'Personal Development Plan' (PDP). It might be structured differently from the material below, but its aim will be the same – to help you describe your achievements and show evidence of your skills. A PDP will include evidence from beyond academic contexts – for example, it might include sports activities or voluntary work – but this chapter will concentrate on academic domains.

It is important to recognise that your academic skills do not simply spring into life when you start a degree programme, however. You have been developing these skills for some time, and you may well be able to provide some good evidence for the aspects below from the academic work you have already done up to now.

Employers want evidence of the following:

- *Self-reliance*. These skills are about your ability to plan activities on your own initiative and carry them out, to be purposeful, positive and well motivated. Perseverance is valued – the fact that you don't give up easily – as is the ability to be resourceful, knowing how to move things forward. *Ask yourself*: When have you shown independence and perseverance in your academic work?

- *An ability to relate to others*. This is about how you work with others, your interpersonal skills, your ability to communicate with different sorts of people, using a variety of communication methods. Relational skills, of course, include being able to listen to others and empathise, but also being able to assert yourself and state your case. People need to be able to work in teams, but management roles require leadership skills and the ability to inspire others with your ideas and plans. *Ask yourself*: When have you shown you can work in a team, and when have you been in a leadership role?

- *General employability skills*. Employers want to employ people they can trust and rely on, who are honest and straightforward. Flexibility, good levels of organisation, punctuality, the ability to meet deadlines and take responsibility – in short, demonstrating professional behaviour – are all important skills. *Ask yourself*: When have you shown yourself to be reliable and dependable? When have you had to be well organised and meet deadlines?

- *Specialist skills*. These are the skills that are specific to particular academic areas. It will be difficult for you to identify what these are if you have not yet embarked on a degree programme. To help you, the next section sets out the particular skills that are typically developed on English Language programmes of study. If you are already on a degree programme, try to provide some examples from your academic work for each of the bullet points.

What skills are taught on English Language programmes?

Below is a list of skills identified in the English Language benchmark statement as particularly developed by students who take the subject. The first set of skills are seen as very specific to the subject, while the second set are seen as associated with the subject, but in a more general way:

Set 1: Subject-specific skills

- the ability to formulate a hypothesis, gather evidence, and construct an acceptable argument within the study of English Language;
- knowledge of the metalanguage appropriate for the discipline and the ability to use correctly a recognised formal terminology;
- critical skills in the close reading, description, analysis, or production of texts or discourses;
- ability to articulate knowledge and understanding of texts, concepts and theories relating to English and to the language faculty more broadly;
- responsiveness to the central role of language in the creation of meaning and a sensitivity to the affective power of language;
- awareness of the variety of Englishes in the world and intercultural awareness.

Set 2: Generic skills

- advanced literacy and communication skills and the ability to apply these in appropriate contexts, including the ability to construct and present coherent, concise and sustained arguments;
- competence in the planning and execution of presentations, project reports, essays and other formal writing;
- the ability to abstract and synthesise information, and to organise the results appropriately;
- the ability to analyse data, and to express the results of that analysis cogently and concisely;
- the ability to draft and redraft texts to achieve clarity of expression and exposition, and to produce a register and style appropriate to the context;
- the ability to assess the merits and demerits of contrasting theories and explanations, including those of other disciplines;
- the ability to think and reason critically, to evaluate evidence and argumentation, and to form a critical judgement of one's own work as well as the work of others, both in academic and non-academic domains;

- the ability to recognise problems and to develop problem-solving strategies;
- the ability to acquire complex data and information of diverse kinds from a variety of sources, including libraries, the internet, corpora, independent fieldwork and data collection;
- bibliographic skills appropriate to the discipline, including accurate citation of sources and consistent use of conventions in the presentation of professional and scholarly work;
- skills in accessing and manipulating data electronically, as well as a broad familiarity with information technology resources;
- effective time management and organisational skills, including the ability to work to a deadline and to handle a number of distinct projects simultaneously.

Too much information? Then try this

This is the summary from the Preface. You should now know how an English Language course can help you to develop these employability skills.

Critical skills

A workplace needs employees who can stand back from what is going on and take an analytical view – that is a critical skill fundamental to research in English Language. Researching something in an organisation – for example, how processes work, or how to change a system, or how to start a new project – entails a number of steps. The first step is some critical thinking in order to work out what the research question is. English Language students are used to dealing with complexity, and looking at issues from different angles, because issues of language are complex and the whole subject is interdisciplinary.

Data collection skills

English Language students know about data, in all its forms. Working with human participants and looking at aspects of communication requires an understanding of the different sources of information that can be called 'data'. English Language students have particular awareness of different types of text, and skills in how to sort and sift information, understanding that there is no one version of 'the truth'.

Presentation skills

If English Language study teaches us anything, it is about the power of language to construct views and attitudes. In studying processes of language understanding and how different texts and discourses work, English Language students are well placed to put their insights to use in their own presentations. They should be particularly skilled in constructing cogent arguments and aware of the language aspects of new communication technologies.

Communication skills

Presenting ideas counts as communication, but there are other aspects to communication as well. Listening skills are very important, not just in order to hear others' views, but in order to understand why they hold those views. English Language students become expert at 'reading between the lines' of what is said and what is meant. This is a key skill for negotiations.

Intercultural skills

English Language students know how language and culture are strongly connected, and how many assumptions can be in play when people interact. In our globalised world, different cultural groups are in contact as never before. Changes to the English language itself are underway as new varieties emerge from these new levels of connectedness. If anyone can help us understand the communication processes of our contemporary world, it's a student of English Language.

Further reading

Particular modules and programmes will of course make their own recommendations for readings, so this chapter will simply offer some suggestions for possible next steps.

The books that have been asterisked in the References are examples of texts that are either specifically aimed at beginning undergraduates, or at non-specialist readers at any level. Many are introductory, aiming to give an overview of a particular area. In some cases, the asterisked books are part of a series, so it is worth mentioning the respective series' names rather than listing individual books and authors:

The Routledge *Intertext* series is a language based-collection currently of 23 individual titles that cover language use in specific contexts – for example, comics, sport, work, advertising, politics, newspapers, magazines, new technologies – as well as larger-scale dimensions such as gender, region and language change. There is also a central book entitled *Working with Texts*, which covers the different 'levels' of language that an analysis might need to refer to.

The Routledge *English Language Introductions* are more substantial texts covering fields of language study, for example, Sociolinguistics, Psycholinguistics, Stylistics, World Englishes, and the Media.

Some book series are very explicitly interdisciplinary, for example, the Routledge *Interface* series focuses on the connections between language and literature. There are also single texts, such as Pope's (1998) *The English Studies Book*, whose starting point is the inextricability of language and literature, seeing these areas as parts of a whole 'English Studies' framework rather than as separate subjects. Texts on Creative Writing, such as *The Creative Writing Handbook* by Singleton and Luckhurst (1999) will, of their very nature, be focusing on both language and literature, in thinking about the creative outputs of language use. And there are new theoretical areas bridging language and literature, for example, Text World Theory within Stylistics, which describes cognitive approaches to text:

Gavins, J. (2007) *Text World Theory: An Introduction*. Edinburgh: Edinburgh University Press.
Singleton, J. and Luckhurst, M. (1999) *The Creative Writing Handbook*. Basingstoke: Palgrave.

As well as single texts and book series, there are some other types of publication that can support English language study, but it is important to understand their nature. The handbook by Singleton and Luckhurst is a mixture of critical views and practical applications, and this tends to characterise those texts that are called 'handbooks'. The idea is that they act as a kind of 'how-to' guide as well as offering theoretical frameworks. Although the idea of handbooks is a good one, you need to be prepared to encounter many different writers, as handbooks are often collections of essays and articles by different people. Although this means that coverage of different areas will be good, there may be some variability in writing styles and accessibility.

There are further types of book that are also collections of one kind or another. For example, there are books that are, rather confusingly, called 'readers' – such as Routledge's *Language and Cultural Theory Reader* (Burke *et al.* 2000). This reader is part of series called *The Politics of Language*. Another example is *The Feminist Critique of Language: A Reader* (Cameron 1998). While these two examples are very useful texts, it is important to realise that readers differ from handbooks in that they often include important articles and extracts from the past, from figures who are thought to have been very influential in the development of the subject. In readers, then, you need to be prepared for some historical perspectives on the academic area you are reading about, not just contemporary views. The role of the editor(s) is to help you set the different articles in context, and understand more about the changes that have occurred in the subject area.

Burke, L., Crowley, T., and Girvin, A. (eds) (2000) *Language and Cultural Theory Reader*. London: Routledge.

Cameron, D. (ed.). (1998) *The Feminist Critique of Language: A Reader* London: Routledge.

Final examples of multiple-entry books are, of course, encyclopedias and dictionaries of various kinds. David Crystal's encyclopedias are well known (from Cambridge University Press), and there are others, such as:

Malmkjaer, K. (ed.) (2011) *Linguistics Encyclopedia*, 3rd edn. London: Routledge.
Wales, K. (2001) *Dictionary of Stylistics*. Harlow: Longman.

There are some areas of growth and change in English Language study that deserve a special mention. The collection and analysis of spoken language have always posed particular challenges, so it is interesting to see new formats being used, such as *Voices in the UK: Accents and Dialects of English*, produced in 2011 as an audiobook from the British Library Sound Archive. There are now many more texts on how to approach the analysis of spoken language, such as the following:

Cameron, D. (2001) *Working with Spoken Discourse*. London: Sage.

Corpora of speech data have also generated new insights on how spoken language works, such as the following text (with optional CDs) which arose from a corpus of casual speech called CANCODE (Cambridge and Nottingham Corpus of Discourse in English):

Carter, R. and McCarthy, M. (1997) *Exploring Spoken English*. Cambridge: Cambridge University Press.

A Routledge series called *Domains of Discourse* specialises in the analysis of speech in particular contexts, for example:

Koester, A. (2006) *Investigating Workplace Discourse*. London: Routledge.
Walsh, S. (2011) *Exploring Classroom Discourse*. London: Routledge.

Working on corpora is in itself a new area of skill, and there are useful new texts that cover this emerging field, for example:

Adolphs, S. (2012) *Multi-modal Spoken Corpus Analysis*. London: Routledge.

New technologies will clearly continue to be an interesting area for the analysis of language use, challenging many of our traditional academic concepts of spoken and written language. Students of English Language need to be able to stand back from the immediacy of their language use and understand some of the issues that lie behind these new contexts for language study. The following books offer useful starting points for that process:

Gane, N. and Beer, D. (2008) *New Media: The Key Concepts*. Oxford: Berg.
Goddard, A. and Geesin, B. (2011) *Language and Technology*. London: Routledge.
Thurlow, C., Lengel, L. and Tomic, A. (2004) *Computer Mediated Communication: An Introduction to Social Interaction Online*. London: Sage.

Final reference needs to be made to the new international role that is emerging for the English language. Fundamental changes are in process, bring with them not only new varieties of English but a need for new perspectives. The following books chart some of the changes that are underway:

Rubdy, R. and Saraceni, M. (2006) *English in the World: Global Rules, Global Roles*. London: Continuum.
Saraceni, M. (2010) *The Relocation of English: Shifting Paradigms in a Global Era*. Basingstoke: Palgrave.

References

Bakhtin, M. M. (1981) *The Dialogic Imagination*. ed. M. Holquist, trans. C. Emerson and M. Holquist. Austin, TX: University of Texas Press.

Baxter, J. (2009) 'Undergraduate English Language: a subject in search of an identity?', *Liaison*, Issue 2, January.

BBC News Magazine (2011) 'Viewpoint: Why do some Americanisms irritate people?' Available at: http://www.bbc.co.uk/news/14130942.

* Beard, A. (2001) *Texts and Contexts*. London: Routledge.

Berger, P and Luckmann, T. (1966) *The Social Construction of Reality: A Treatise in the Sociology of Knowledge*. New York: Anchor Books.

Bourdieu, P. (1991) *Language and Symbolic Power*. Cambridge, MA: Harvard University Press.

British National Corpus (BNC). Free sample available at: http://corpus.byu.edu/bnc/.

Bullock Report (1975) *A Language for Life*. London: HMSO.

Cameron, D. (1995) *Verbal Hygiene*. London: Routledge.

Cameron, D. (1998) *The Feminist Critique of Language*. London: Routledge.

Carter, A. (1981) 'The company of wolves', in *The Bloody Chamber and Other Stories*. London: Penguin.

Carter Scott, C. (1999) *If Life is a Game, These Are the Rules: 10 Rules for Being Human*. London: Hodder & Stoughton.

* Chandler, D. (2002) *Semiotics: The Basics*. London: Routledge.

Chandler, D. (2006) 'Identities under construction', in J. Maybin (ed.) *The Art of English*. Maidenhead: Open University Press.

Chomsky, N. (1965) *Aspects of the Theory of Syntax*. Cambridge, MA: MIT Press.

Chomsky, N. (1975) *Syntactic Structures*. The Hague: Mouton de Gruyter.

Clark, H. H. (1996) *Using Language*. Cambridge: Cambridge University Press.

Clark, H. H. and Brennan, S. E. (1991) 'Grounding in communication', in L. B. Resnick, J. M. Levine and J. S. D. Teasley (eds) *Perspectives on Socially Shared Cognition*. Washington, DC: American Psychological Association.

Coulthard, M. and Brazil, D. (1992) 'Exchange structure', in M. Coulthard (ed.) *Advances in Spoken Discourse Analysis*. London: Routledge, pp. 50–78.

Covey, S. (1989) *The 7 Habits of Highly Effective People*. New York: Simon & Schuster.

Crowley, T. (2003) *Standard English and the Politics of Language*. Basingstoke: Palgrave.

de Saussure, F. (1974) *Course in General Linguistics*. London: Fontana.

D'Orsey, A. J. D. (1861) *The Study of the English Language:An Essential Part of a University Course*. Cambridge: Deighton, Bell, and Company.

Eaglestone, R. (2002) *Doing English: A Guide for Literature Students,* 2nd edn. London: Routledge.

Fairclough, N. (2001) *Language and Power*. London: Longman.

Fish, S. (1980) *Is There a Text in This Class? The Authority of Interpretive Communities*. Cambridge, MA: Harvard University Press.

Fowler, R. (1996) *Linguistic Criticism*. Oxford: Oxford University Press.

Fox, K. (2005) *Watching the English*. London: Hodder and Stoughton.

Gannes, L. (2011) 'I Can has $30 million: LOLcats become funny business', *Wall Street Journal Digital Network*, January 17. Available at: http://allthingsd.com/20110117/i-can-has-30m-lolcats-become-funny-business/.

* Gee, J. P. (1999) *An Introduction to Discourse Analysis*. London: Routledge.

Geertz, C. (1973) *The Interpretation of Cultures*. New York: Basic Books.

Giles, H., Coupland, J. and Coupland, N. (1991) *Contexts of Accommodation: Developments in Applied Linguistics*. Cambridge: Cambridge University Press.

Goddard, A. (2000) *Researching Language*. Oxford: Heinemann.

Goddard, A. (2003) ' "*Is there anybody out there?*": creative language play and literariness in internet relay chat (IRC)', in A. Schorr, B. Campbell and M. Schenk (eds) *Communication Research and Media Science in Europe*. Berlin: Mouton de Gruyter.

Goddard, A. (2004) ' "*The Way to Write a Phone Call*": multimodality in novices' use and perceptions of interactive written discourse', in R. Scollon and P. Levine (eds) *Georgetown University Round Table on Languages and Linguistics: Discourse Analysis and Technology: Multimodal Discourse Analysis*. Washington, DC: Georgetown University Press.

Goddard, A. (2005) 'Being online', PhD thesis, University of Nottingham.

Goddard, A. (2011) 'Type you soon!' A stylistic approach to language use in a virtual learning environment', *Language and Literature*, 20(3): 184–200.

Goddard, A. and Beard, A. (2007) 'As simple as ABC?: Issues of transition for students of English Language A Level going on to study English Language/Linguistics in Higher Education', *HEA English Subject Centre Report Series*, 14.

* Goddard, A. and Geesin, B. (2011) *Language and Technology*. London: Routledge.

* Goddard, A. and Mean, L. (2009) *Language and Gender*, 2nd edn. London: Routledge.

Goffman, E. (1963) *Behaviour in Public Places*. New York: The Free Press.

Goffman, E. (1969) *The Presentation of Self in Everyday Life.* London: Penguin.

Goffman, E. (1974) *Frame Analysis.* Harmondsworth: Penguin.

Graddol, D. (2006) *English Next: Why Global English May Mean the End of 'English as a Foreign Language'.* British Council. Available at: http://www.britishcouncil.org/learning-research-english-next.pdf (accessed 18 July 2011).

Gumperz, J. (1982) *Discourse Strategies.* Cambridge: Cambridge University Press.

Hall, C., Smith, P. and Wicaksono, R. (2011) *Mapping Applied Linguistics.* London: Routledge.

Halliday, M.A.K. (2004) *An Introduction to Functional Grammar.* London: Hodder.

Halliday, M.A.K. and Hasan, R. (1976) *Cohesion in English.* London: Longman.

Harvey, K, and Shalom, C. (eds) (1997) *Language and Desire: Encoding Sex, Romance and Intimacy.* London: Routledge.

Hoey, M. (2000) *Textual Interaction: An Introduction to Written Discourse Analysis.* London: Routledge.

Hymes, D.H. (1962) 'The ethnography of speaking', in T. Gladwin and W. C. Sturtevant (eds) *Anthropology and Human Behaviour.* Washington, DC: Anthropology Society of Washington.

Johnson, B. S. (1999) *The Unfortunates.* London: Picador.

Katre, S. M. (1987) *Astadhyayi of Panini.* Austin, TX: University of Texas Press.

Kingman Report (1988) *Report of the Committee of Inquiry into the Teaching of English Language.* London: HMSO.

Labov, W. (1966) *The Social Stratification of English in New York City.* Washington, DC: Center for Applied Linguistics.

Labov, W. (1972) *Language in the Inner City: Studies in Black English Vernacular.* Philadelphia: University of Pennsylvania Press.

Lakoff, G. (1987) *Women, Fire and Dangerous Things: What Categories Reveal about the Mind.* Chicago: University of Chicago Press.

Lakoff, G. and Johnson, M. (1980) *Metaphors We Live By.* Chicago: University of Chicago Press.

Madden, M. (2005) *99 Ways to Tell a Story.* London: Penguin.

* McLoughlin, L. (2000) *The Language of Magazines.* London: Routledge.

Miller, C. and Swift, K. (1980) *The Handbook of Non-Sexist Writing.* London: The Women's Press.

Milroy, L. (1987) *Language and Social Networks.* Oxford: Blackwell.

Moi, T. (ed.) (1986) *The Kristeva Reader.* Oxford: Blackwell.

Morgan, G. (1986) *Images of Organization.* London: Sage.

Newbolt Report (1921) *A Report on the Teaching of English in England and Wales.* London: HMSO.

Palmer, F. (1984) *Grammar.* London: Penguin.

* Pope, R. (1995) *Textual Intervention.* London: Routledge.

Rabinow, P. (1991) *The Foucault Reader.* London: Penguin.

Rampton, B. (2002) 'Ritual and foreign language practices at school', *Language in Society* 31(4): 491–525.

Ratcliffe, S. K. (1909) *Bulletin*. London: English Association, 7 February.

* Reeves, C. (2005) *The Language of Science*. London: Routledge.

Rhys, J. (1966) *The Wide Sargasso Sea*. London: Penguin.

Richards, I. A. (1936) *The Meaning of Meaning*. London: Kegan Paul.

Richter, D. (2004) 'Ludwig Wittgenstein', *Internet Encyclopedia of Philosophy*. Available at: http://www.iep.utm.edu/wittgens/.

Robinson, P, and Giles, H. (2011) *The Handbook of Language and Social Psychology*. Oxford: Blackwell.

Sacks, H. (1995) *Lectures on Conversation*, vols I and II, ed. G. Jefferson. Oxford: Blackwell.

Schank, R. and Abelson, R. (1977) *Scripts, Plans, Goals and Understanding*. Mahwah, NJ: Lawrence Erlbaum.

Schiffrin, D. (1987) *Discourse Markers*. Cambridge: Cambridge University Press.

* Scollon, R. and Scollon, S. W. (2003) *Discourses in Place: Language in the Material World*. London: Routledge.

Searle, J. (1969) *Speech Acts*. Cambridge: Cambridge University Press.

Shawcross, Mr. (1909) *Bulletin*. London: English Association, 7 February.

Simpson, P. (1993) *Language, Ideology and Point of View*. London: Routledge.

* Simpson, P. (2004) *Stylistics: A Resource Book for Students*. London: Routledge.

Spender, D. (1980) *Man Made Language*. London: The Women's Press.

Sperber, D. and Wilson, D. (1995) *Relevance: Communication and Cognition*. Oxford: Blackwell.

Stephens, W. B. (1998) *Education in Britain, 1750–1914*. Basingstoke: Palgrave Macmillan.

* Street, B. and Lefstein, A. (2007) *Literacy: An Advanced Resource Book for Students*. London: Routledge.

Swales, J. (1998) *Other Floors, Other Voices: A Textography of a Small University Building*. Mahwah, NJ: Lawrence Erlbaum.

Tajfel, H. ([1982] 2010) *Social Identity and Intergroup Relations*. Cambridge: Cambridge University Press.

Thurlow, C. and Jaworski, A. (2006) 'The alchemy of the upwardly mobile: symbolic capital and the stylization of elites in frequent-flyer programmes', *Discourse & Society*, 17(1): 131–67.

Thynne, J. (2010) 'They came, they soared, they conquered', *The Independent*, 2 September.

* Toolan, M. (2001) *Narrative: A Critical Linguistic Introduction*, 2nd edn. London: Routledge.

Trask, R. L. (1999) *Key Concepts in Language and Linguistics*. London: Routledge.

Trudgill, P. (1978) *The Social Differentiation of English in Norwich*. Cambridge: Cambridge University Press.

Wells, J. C. (1982) *Accents of English*. Cambridge: Cambridge University Press.

Wittgenstein, L. (1961) *Tractatus Logico-Philosophicus*, trans. D. F. Pears and B. F. McGuinness. London: Routledge.

Links to UK benchmarks

The English Language Benchmarks can be found at: http://www.english.heacademy. ac.uk/explore/resources/language/docs/EL_benchmarking_final.pdf.

Other subject benchmarks can be found at: http://www.qaa.ac.uk/ASSURINGST ANDARDSANDQUALITY/SUBJECT-GUIDANCE/Pages/Subject-benchmark-statements.aspx.

This link is to *Prospects* – the UK's official graduate careers website: http://www. prospects.ac.uk/what_do_graduates_do_about_data.htm.

This link is to the 2010 report, 'What Do Graduates Do?' (HECSU/AGCAS). http:// www.prospects.ac.uk/assets/assets/documents/wdgd_2010.pdf.

Index of terms

This is a form of combined glossary and index. Listed below are some of the key terms used in the book, together with brief definitions for purposes of reference. The page references will normally take you to the first use of the term in the book, where it will be shown in bold.

active voice   62

The same idea or event can be expressed in different ways in English sentences depending on whether the verb is used in the active, or passive voice. This choice refers to the form in which a verb appears, and to the order of elements in a sentence. The result is to change the emphasis within a sentence. The first example below uses the active voice, and the second example the passive voice. You can see how although the two sentences describe the same action (biting) and participants (a dog and a man), the positioning of the elements produces a different emphasis in each case. Also, in the second example, the agent phrase (in brackets) can be omitted. Passive sentences can leave out the person or thing responsible for an action:

> The dog bit the man
> The man was bitten (by the dog)

adverbials   57

Language items that give more information about verbs, specifically where, when, and how activities were performed or states of being were realised.

competence   36
In Chomskyan analysis, the abstract language system itself – similar to de
Saussure's idea of '*la langue*'.

conceptual metaphor   41
A group of metaphors that collectively elaborate ways of thinking about a
particular topic.

concordance   21
A computer-based program that allows a corpus of data to be searched
and which produces the sought item in the context of where it occurred in
sentences or utterances. See *corpus*.

connotations   19
The connotations of a word are the associations it creates.

construction grammar   88
A system of analysis which takes a series of grammatical constructions as the
base units of their approach.

convergence   31
In language study, a marked shift in style to indicate solidarity with another.

conversation analysis   19
A field of analysis which is interested in how conversation is organised.

corpora   111
See corpus.

corpus   21
In language study, a collection of data held on a computer and tagged, in order
to be searchable in different ways. The term 'corpus' is Latin for 'body', so
this refers to a body of material. The plural is 'corpora'.

critical   47
An approach which involves an examination of society and culture in its
analysis.

critical discourse analysis   47
An approach which explicitly addresses issues of power and domination by
showing how social inequalities are reproduced in the texts and discourses
around us.

cultural studies   62
The study of contemporary culture, using a range of approaches, but focusing
particularly on aspects of ideology and on how messages are communicated.

deficit model   31
In language study, the idea that the language people use is to blame for their lack of success in acquiring power in society. More broadly, a focus on what people cannot do, rather than what they can do.

descriptive   88
An approach that takes language as it is actually used as the starting point for evidence of what should be seen as 'correct' or 'standard'. Beyond discussions of standardisation, a descriptive approach attempts to describe occurrences of language use and this approach is sometimes contrasted with more theoretical approaches that try to build abstract models.

deterministic   8
In language study, determinism describes the idea that aspects of language cause or produce certain effects, for example, that language determines thought.

diachronic   8
Study of language historically, across time.

dialect   20
Language that is characteristic of a particular geographical region.

dialectology   30
The study of patterns of regional language use.

discourse analysis   18
In language study, this can mean either the analysis of spoken interactions, or the analysis of how different topics are discussed across texts of all kinds.

discourse markers   81
Linguistic items that enable participants to comment on the ongoing discourse, for example, saying 'briefly' means that you are going to give a summary or shortened version.

discourses   25
Repeated ways of talking or writing about a topic or idea.

divergence   31
In language study, a marked shift in style in order to signal social distance from another.

dramaturgical   18
Drawing on the field of drama and performance.

empirical 106
An approach based on the collection of observable evidence alone.

estuary English 31
An accent from the South-east of England, called 'estuary' in reference to the River Thames. This accent has been seen to rival RP as a newer prestige variety in recent times.

etymology 21
Study of the derivations of words and phrases, for example, which languages they came from originally and what the terms have meant historically.

feminist 66
An approach concerned with establishing and defending equal treatment for women. Feminist analysis is not just about analysing texts associated with women, as the feminist aim of gender equality cannot be achieved without considering how men are represented and defined.

field 46
As used by the linguist Michael Halliday, field refers to the topic or subject being discussed in an interaction or text. 'Semantic field' is a more general term used in linguistics for language which relates to a particular domain of language use.

first person narrative 58
A story told using first person pronouns, offering internal views.

first person pronoun 58
'I' (singular) or 'we' (plural).

folksonomy 80
A form of collaborative online categorisation where individuals 'tag' content with keywords. Examples are YouTube and Flickr. Folksonomies are searchable databases that allow for a variety of categories created by the users.

forensics 9
The application of science to legal problems and cases.

formality 19
A level of language use which refers to a particular social context or situation. Formal language is used in social situations which are distant and more impersonal; informal language is used in social situations which are intimate and casual.

frames   18

As used by Erving Goffman and analysts following his approach, frames operate within interactions to distinguish one kind of activity from another, for example, dividing 'play' from 'non-play'. The concept can be likened to a picture frame, which draws a boundary round something which is then viewed in a certain way.

functional   44

Focused on language functions.

gender   31

Gender refers to socially expected characteristics rather than biological ones. For example, while having ovaries is a biological characteristic (of sex), being interested in babies is a socially expected characteristic (of gender). There are ongoing disputes about what is the result of sex (biology) and what of gender (society).

generative grammar   35

A theory of grammar developed by Noam Chomsky, which proposed different levels of structure to explain how individuals processed and produced a wide range of utterances from a finite set of rules.

genre   5

A type of text or discourse with characteristic and recognisable features.

graphological   85

The visual aspects of written language, such as layout and typeface.

grapho-phonemic   68

The relationship between written symbols (graphemes) and sounds (phonemes)

hypercorrection   83

Over-correction as a result of trying to apply a rule too generally. For example, someone who would not normally use an /h/ sound before initial vowels (for example, in a word like 'hospital') might worry about seeming incorrect, and so add an /h/ inappropriately before all initial vowels, producing 'happles' and 'horanges' as a result. See *shibboleth*.

hypothesis   8

A proposed explanation.

A lexeme is a cluster of all the variants of a lexical item – for example, 'run', 'runs' and 'running' are not seen as separate, unrelated words but as variants of the same lexeme. The base form – the form that is usually at the beginning of a dictionary citation – is termed a lemma. In this case, it would be 'run'.

Lexis refers to the vocabulary of a language.

A language that is used for mutual communication in contexts where it is no-one's first language. The term originally meant 'the language of the Franks', which was a mixed language (mainly Italian and French) used for communication and trade in medieval times.

Analysis of literary texts – how they work, what they mean, their interrelationships, etc.

A departure from what is expected, or from the 'norm' of usage.

An experimental research design where the same speaker assumes different accents, or 'guises'.

Language that describes language itself.

A way of linking two items or ideas together where there is no logical connection or literal truth. For example, if you say 'we've come to the end of the road in this relationship', you are likening relationships to journeys.

Elements of language that offer more information about other items.

The smallest meaningful unit of a language.

multimodal 78
Operating in more than one mode at the same time. Many types of computer-based communication are multimodal, in that they combine characteristics of writing (for example, being composed on a keyboard) with those of speech (for example, operating in real time).

narratee 57
The person who appears to be being addressed by a text.

narrative 50
A text which has a story-like construction involving a sequence of events.

narrator 22
The apparent 'voice' or persona telling a story.

neurolinguistics 32
The neurological (nerve cell) basis of language in the brain.

noun 87
A noun names a person, thing or idea.

object 117
See subject.

orthographic 68
Related to the spelling system.

overextension 39
The over-application of a rule beyond what is appropriate.

passive voice 62
See active voice.

performance 36
In Chomskyan analysis, this refers to the actual language produced by people on an everyday basis – similar to de Saussure's '*la parole*'.

philology 3
A type of study popular in the nineteenth century focusing on the historical development of languages via written sources.

phoneme 83
A single unit of sound.

phoneticians 31
Researchers who specialise in phonetics.

broadly to describe persuasive language that uses certain strategies and features.

salient   37
Meaningful, noteworthy, requiring attention.

Sapir–Whorf hypothesis   8
Named after the American anthropological linguists, Edward Sapir and Benjamin Lee Whorf, the hypothesis proposes that language constructs ways of viewing the world.

schemas   43
Psychologically based constructs and connections which allow us to understand the nature of events in a known culture.

scripts   43
From the field of artificial intelligence, the idea of scripts is that particular contexts and roles generate predictable routines, therefore predictable uses of language. Scripting in this sense has obvious connections with dramatic roles, where an author has already set down the words that characters will say.

semantics   43
At a micro-level, semantics refers to the meanings of words and phrases. But at a macro-level, it can also mean the overall meaning of a text or event.

semiology   7
The study of sign systems, including language. This was de Saussure's original term for the proposed area, but in many cases nowadays people tend to use the term 'semiotics' to mean the same thing.

semiotics   7
The study of sign systems and their meanings, ranging from the smallest logo to entire films or events.

sense relations   43
Relationships between words, for example synonymy (terms that are equivalent).

shibboleth   16
A term from the Hebrew Bible (*Judges*, Chapter 12) meaning 'ear of corn'. The word was used as a test by the Gileadites to reveal the identity of Ephraimites, who had been conquered and were trying to escape without notice. Ephraimites had no /ʃ/ sound in their language, so would have said

'Sibboleth' rather than 'Shibboleth'. The term in modern usage now means a 'test word' or 'test marker', signalling one's group identity.

signs 62
A sign is 'something that has significance'. In semiotics, a sign is made up of the 'signifier' (the item communicating) and the 'signified' (what it is understood to mean).

singular 25
A grammatical coding meaning a single individual is being referred to.

slang 20
Slang is informal language that particular groups, such as interest groups, use to identify themselves. It is different from regional dialect and also from colloquial, informal language in general.

social constructivist 19
The view that reality is to a large extent socially constructed by the members of the culture.

social identity theory 31
A theory developed by Henry Tajfel to explain why individuals identify themselves as part of a social group and espouse group values.

spatio-temporal 57
Relating to space and time.

speech act theory 44
A type of theory which saw language as action, thus it classified language uses according to the respective actions performed by them.

speech and language therapy 9
The treatment of speech disorders and language disorders.

standardisation 24
The process of devising a common code or practice.

stereotypes 31
Generalised attributes which are associated with individuals on the basis of their group membership.

stress 84
A form of emphasis in speech, making a sound or group of sounds more prominent.

structural   44
Focused on language structures.

structuralism   62
An approach which sees meaning as derived from the idea that items are in a system and defined as much by their differences as their similarities.

style shifting   31
Making changes within ongoing communication to the type of language being chosen, for example, changing the level of formality.

suprasegmental   83
Features of spoken language that occur across stretches of sound rather than on individual segments.

subject   25
Grammatically, the subject is the person or thing that is carrying out the action of the verb. Verbs can also refer to states of feeling or being, so this definition is a basic starting point. The person or thing on the receiving end of actions or processes is called the grammatical *object*.

symbolic   24
Suggesting associations rather than referring to something directly.

synchronic   8
Study of language across society with a focus on a contemporary time.

synonyms   20
Terms which have equivalent meanings.

syntactic   34
Syntax governs how sentences are structured, for example, there are significant syntactic rules about word order in English.

systemic-functional grammar   88
A system of grammatical analysis developed by Michael Halliday which attempts to relate aspects of the language system to the social functions of language use.

taboo   100
The idea that some areas of experience are off-limits to mention, and have to be avoided or described using a 'polite' term (called a euphemism). The term taboo is based on a Polynesian word, 'tabu', which refers to holy ground that cannot be walked on.

theoretical linguistics 35
This area is concerned with developing models of linguistic knowledge. It is sometimes contrasted with applied linguistics or descriptive linguistics.

third person narrative 58
A story told from an apparently objective vantage point, describing things and other people by using third person pronouns.

third person pronoun 58
'He', 'she', 'it' (singular) or 'they' (plural).

tropes 101
Figurative language, such as metaphor, where meaning operates on more than one level.

variation 16
In language study, variationist research focuses on the differences between groups of language users, or compares a particular group with a 'norm' or standard pattern of usage.

verb 87
A verb encodes actions, processes or states of being, for example, 'jump', 'appear'.

voice 62
In phonetics, a sound is called 'voiced' if it is produced via vibration of the vocal cords. Without this vibration, the sound is termed 'voiceless'. For use of the term 'voice' in grammatical contexts, see *active voice*, *passive voice*.

world Englishes 26
The different versions of the English language that are used around the world as official, semi-official, or widespread forms of communication within countries, particularly those countries that were former colonies of the UK.

x-bar theory 35
A theory which tries to specify a set of universal rules for syntactic structures across all languages.